Wesleyan Essentials IN A Multicultural SOCIETY

Ted A. Campbell AND
Michael T. Burns

Abingdon Press
Nashville

WESLEYAN ESSENTIALS IN A MULTICULTURAL SOCIETY

Copyright © 2004 by Abingdon Press

All rights reserved.

This book is printed on acid-free paper.

Library of Congress Cataloging in Publication Data

Campbell, Ted.
  Wesleyan essentials in a multicultural society / Ted A. Campbell, Michael T. Burns.
    p. cm.
  ISBN 0-687-03994-0 (alk. paper)
  1. Methodist Church—Doctrines. 2. Multiculturalism—Religious aspects—Methodist Church. 3. Holiness churches—Doctrines. 4. Multiculturalism—Religious aspects—Holiness churches. I. Burns, Michael T. II. Title.

  BX8331.3.C36 2004
  287—dc22

           2003024257

04 05 06 07 08 09 10 11 12 13 – 10 9 8 7 6 5 4 3 2 1

MANUFACTURED IN THE UNITED STATES OF AMERICA

Contents

CHAPTER 1

The Challenge
of Multiculturalism

*Beloved, while eagerly preparing to write to you about the
salvation we share, I find it necessary to write and appeal to
you to contend for the faith that was once for all entrusted
to the saints.* (Jude 1-3)

Introduction

We are challenged "to contend for the faith that was once for all
entrusted to the saints" in the context of a multicultural society. It is
a daunting challenge. Beliefs we once thought universal, and
authorities (like the Bible) to which we once appealed as givens,
cannot be taken for granted. It is also an exciting challenge. Christ
has called us to "make disciples of all nations, baptizing them in the
name of the Father and of the Son and of the Holy Spirit" (Matthew
28:19). This challenge no longer requires a passport or a visa: "the
nations" are near at hand. This study series considers the challenge
of contending for the Christian faith and the historic Wesleyan mission in the context of contemporary, multicultural society.

A Multicultural Society and Its Challenges
to Christian Belief

In a sense, **a multicultural society is not a new thing**. The
conquests of Alexander the Great, in the 300s B.C., brought about a

Near Eastern society that embraced many conquered nations and their cultures: Persia, Egypt, Judah, and others. Sophisticated people in the kingdoms established by Alexander's generals liked to think of themselves as cosmopolitans, that is, world citizens. The Roman Empire built on Alexander's conquests and brought even more nations and cultures into its empire. More recently, the British Empire of the nineteenth century embraced a great number of the world's peoples and cultures. The bare fact that many cultures have been forced together is not a new thing. But in the past, when cultures were forced together, there was **a dominant culture** in each of these multicultural societies: the Hellenistic culture of Alexander's kingdoms, the Latin culture of ancient Rome, the Victorian culture of the British Empire in the late 1800s. Some would say that American (or U.S.) culture became the globally dominant culture in the late twentieth century as a result of commercial expansion.

Something new has happened since the early 1900s. **The notion of a dominant Western culture was seriously challenged** in the first place **by non-Western peoples**. The Boxer Rebellion in 1900 in China, which resulted in the killing of many Christian missionaries, signaled the violent rejection of the notion of Western cultural superiority. Mohandas Gandhi's challenge to British rule in India marked a nonviolent and morally disciplined rejection of Western cultural dominance. These patterns were repeated through the twentieth century. Native peoples consistently rejected Western political, economic, cultural, and (most important for this study) religious institutions as alien to their own traditions. This does not mean that there ceased to be a dominant culture, but it means that the global dominance of Western culture was seriously challenged.

Moreover, **Western peoples began to question their own cultural superiority** in the twentieth century. This could be seen early on in anthropological studies. The Polish-born British anthropologist Bronislaw Malinowski went to the Trobriand Islands in the Pacific between 1914 and 1918. He attempted to see the world through the eyes of native peoples, and his field investigations revolutionized anthropological studies. No longer did investigators presume the inferiority of native peoples, but tried instead to understand non-Western peoples on their own terms. Within a few decades, this anthropological perspective had begun to influence Western philosophy and culture much more broadly.

One area in which this suspicion of Western cultural superiority appeared was in new forms of **philosophy** in the twentieth century. Western philosophies since the Enlightenment (1600s and 1700s) had insisted on the superiority of reason and observation as the surest ways of knowing about the world. Later beliefs about Western cultural superiority were grounded in the Western world's rational and scientific enterprises. By the early decades of the twentieth century, however, philosophers had begun to question these Enlightenment suppositions. The career of the philosopher Ludwig **Wittgenstein** illustrates the transition from a philosophy that presupposed one right way of knowing to a philosophy that stressed the multiplicity of ways in which humans know about the world. In Wittgenstein's later thought, one must understand the complexity of our uses of language in which meaning is embedded.

The **implications of this philosophy**—and Wittgenstein's later thought served as the basis for many Western philosophies in the twentieth century—is crucial: What is "true" from one perspective may not be "true" from another perspective. Even the sneering quotation marks around the word "true" illustrate the ambiguity involved in such a view of the world. This philosophical turn fitted nicely with the growing trend in anthropology and elsewhere to reconsider the traditions and wisdom of non-Western peoples.

But it isn't just philosophers who have been concerned about universal or absolute truths. The point must not be missed that **the suspicion of claims to universal truth has affected Western culture deeply** since the early twentieth century. Claims to universal truth are often greeted with a suspicion of arrogance. Christian traditionalists may see their suspicious contemporaries as advocating a kind of "anything goes" attitude to life. Our suspicious contemporaries, however, often see their own skepticism as a moral principle. They point out that claims to universal or absolute truth in the past amount to a kind of bigotry that has justified horrendous human suffering and destruction. Their point cannot be neglected. Dominant cultures, and their religious leaders, have often perpetrated hideous evil.

7

The challenge of multiculturalism, then, is not only the challenge of a society in which many cultures coexist. For us, it is the challenge of making sense of the Christian faith, "the faith that was once for all entrusted to the saints," in a society where all claims to absolute truth are met with serious suspicion. It is the challenge of giving "an accounting for the hope that is in" us (1 Peter 3:15) to people who fear that their own traditions and customs will be destroyed by the claims of Christian faith. The challenge of multiculturalism is the challenge of proclaiming Christ in a world where Christian cultural dominance is a fading memory.

Problems with Multiculturalism and Relativism

Multiculturalism and the challenge of openness to the world's various claims of truth and wisdom raise a number of problems. For one thing, it is **practically** difficult to maintain a kind of absolute openness to all claims to truth. Despite the positive tone of his field reports, Malinowski's private diaries frequently reveal his contempt for the natives of the Trobriand Islands. A frequent motif in postmodern literature (and humor) is the point at which an observer's pretended objectivity gives way to a more honest expression of their impressions.

Moreover, although the attempt to understand other persons and cultures empathetically has become foundational for the social sciences (sociology, psychology, and anthropology) and for studies of art and literature, **it has not won broad acceptance in the hard sciences** (such as chemistry, physics, or biology). Scientific revolutions may come about when an old perspective gives way to a new one, but many scientists are reluctant to concede that the truth as seen from one perspective must be as helpful (or even as true) as the truth seen from any other perspective.

At the level of philosophical discussion, the problems with multiculturalism are often dealt with as responses to **relativism**. Relativism responds to claims of universal or absolute truth with the counterclaim that all truth is relative. That is, all claims are relative to the perspective of the cultural system, the linguistic system, and the particular historical context in which truths are expressed. But what is the status of the claim that "all truth is relative"? It appears to be an absolute claim, and if that is true, then it bears its own contradiction. New absolutes simply replace old ones.

A broader problem raised by multiculturalism is **the sense that we lack bearings or foundations** in contemporary society. On what grounds do we build a truly multicultural society? Could we build it on the greatest common denominator of all the cultures we find in any given place or country? What if the greatest common denominator isn't much? What if its values conflict fundamentally with the values of a particular subculture (like historic Christianity)? More practically, how do we raise and form children morally, especially in public institutions, when there is not a broad agreement on cultural and moral foundations? These questions have a tendency to push persons either to reject the multicultural society as a whole, or to seek common ground.

In fact, one of the most problematic of responses to multiculturalism has been **its tendency to encourage people to reject culture and society at large and to retreat into their own subcultures**. Although multiculturalism might lead some people to try to understand each other better, it leads others to despair and the sense that it is impossible to understand persons of other cultural backgrounds than oneself. Not surprisingly, many forms of **cultural fundamentalism** (Islamic, Hindu, and Christian) have arisen in response to contemporary multicultural societies. Common to them is the radical rejection of any possibility of compromise with, or even understanding of, persons outside of their own cultural traditions.

Paul on Mars Hill

The previous paragraph suggests one possible response to the challenge of multiculturalism, and that is the response of **Christian fundamentalism**. Christian fundamentalism often claims that the Western world is in fact superior to other cultures because of its Christian cultural grounding. Fundamentalists see Western modernism, including the move to a multicultural society, as a sign of decline in civilization, and call for a vigorous reassertion of Christian values as they have been historically expressed in Western societies. Fundamentalism in this sense obviously comes at a high cost: it means, essentially, abandoning contemporary society as hopeless and retreating into a Christian enclave.

At the opposite end of the spectrum from fundamentalism is **religious syncretism**, a blending of cultural and religious traditions grounded in the belief that no one religious tradition has a monopoly on the truth. On this view, we should choose what is valuable from each tradition, but reject their exclusive claims. One obvious problem with religious syncretism is that it requires religious persons to abandon the most distinctive claims of their own religious traditions, namely, the ultimate or final claims that religious traditions make. Another problem is that, just as relativism ends up creating new absolutes, so religious syncretism ends up creating new religions. It is difficult, if not impossible, to reconcile the integrity of any religious tradition with religious syncretism.

Most Christians have historically lived and taught the Christian faith avoiding the extremes of religious fundamentalism and religious syncretism. But **older models for relating Christian faith to our culture, such as Protestant liberalism, seem hardly adequate today.** Liberalism offered an intimate compromise between Protestant faith and modern Western culture. But for this very reason, older forms of liberalism were closely tied to the notion of Western cultural superiority. Classical Western liberalism fails as a response to a multicultural society.

We are in a very different place today. Perhaps we find ourselves today in the position of **Paul as he visited** the very cosmopolitan, very multicultural ancient city of **Athens**: "I went through the city and looked carefully at the objects of your worship" (Acts 17:23*a*), he said to the Athenians. He went on to quote a couple of Greek poets to the crowd there. He found an altar with the inscription *agnostōi theōi*, "to an unknown god." And there on Mars Hill (the *Areopagus*) he delivered his point: "What therefore you worship as unknown, this I proclaim to you" (Acts 17:23*b*).

Paul's words to the Athenians give us **two important clues** for Christian engagement in a multicultural society. **First**, his words show that **Christians are called to engage the cultures around them**. Paul did not retreat from the world and its cultures. He went to the Areopagus in Athens; he "looked carefully" at the shrines there, he knew enough of Greek language and Hellenistic literature to be able to quote it in speaking to the Athenians. Second, Paul's words show that **Christians are called to proclaim Christ with integrity** in our multicultural context. Paul's gospel was no syncretistic compromise with Hellenistic religion. He carried out on Mars Hill his promise to proclaim "to those who are the called, both Jews and Greeks, Christ the power of God and the wisdom of God" (1 Corinthians 1:24). We are called, then, to engage the world around us with the authentic message of the gospel.

The Christian Faith and the Wesleyan Mission

As United Methodists or Wesleyan Christians, we should be clear not to confuse Methodism or Wesleyanism with the gospel. United Methodists are Christians first, and **the Wesleyan mission is a particular form or expression of the Christian message**. But it is an expression of the Christian message that may bear particular relevance in our consideration of the Christian faith in a multicultural society. Let us examine here three reasons why the Wesleyan expression of Christian faith has relevance for our multicultural society.

First, the Wesleyan understanding of Christian faith involves a rich understanding of God's gifts to the whole world. John Wesley, and later Methodists, consistently taught that divine grace is available to all persons in the world. Christ is "the true light, which enlightens everyone" (John 1:9). This did not mean that everyone would be saved, but that a preparatory (or prevenient) grace had been given to all people. When John Wesley visited Georgia as a missionary of the Society for the Propagation of the Gospel, he conducted lengthy interviews with Native American people, inquiring about their own religious and moral beliefs. This was consistent with his understanding that grace was given to all people. Just as Paul considered carefully the religious shrines of the Athenians, so Wesleyans are called to consider carefully the religious and cultural traditions of other peoples.

11

Second, the Wesleyan understanding of the gospel involves the claim that our own culture and society, as well as others, stands under God's judgment. John Wesley once preached a sermon on "The General Spread of the Gospel." In the first paragraphs of this sermon he condemned the ignorance and superstition of heathen people, then he condemned the wickedness of Muslims and even of Eastern Christians. Imagine his eighteenth-century hearers applauding his attacks on the heathen, the Muslim, the distant Eastern Christians. But the sermon then takes a turn that Wesley's hearers may not have anticipated. He moves on to a stunning condemnation of Western Christians—or at least, those in the Western world who pretended to be Christians. This was not a new preaching technique: the prophet Amos had tried it long ago, condemning all the nations around Israel, then zooming in with his condemnation of his own people. Wesley's sermon was not at all a vindication of Western superiority; in fact, he described the corruptions of other peoples to drive home his point that his own society also stood in desperate need of divine grace. If we are to be Wesleyans in the midst of a multicultural society, we should be willing to acknowledge the corruption and decadence of our own society and culture.

Third, the Wesleyan understanding of the gospel makes a clear distinction between what is essential for the Christian faith, and what is nonessential. In the midst of inter-Christian divisions in England, John Wesley preached a sermon on a "Catholic Spirit." In this sermon, he made the claim that Christians may differ on any number of opinions, but need to be united in the "essentials" of the Christian faith. In other places, he made clear what he held these Christian essentials to be. For example, belief in the final authority of the Scripture (the subject of chapter 2) or belief in the Holy Trinity (the subject of chapter 3) were essentials of Christian teaching in Wesley's view. Particular customs of worship, however, he held to be "opinions" rather than essentials. This study series examines the notion of "essential doctrines" or teachings as a way of being clear about the meaning of the Christian faith in a contemporary, multicultural society.

Talking the Talk and Walking the Walk

"May you live in interesting times." Some say that this expression was originally a curse; we should take it as a blessing. We do live in interesting times. As you drive along the streets or walk in the shopping mall, think of Paul on Mars Hill ("the objects of your devotion . . . "). The people you see and meet will seldom take it for granted that Christianity (or any other tradition) is the basis for life today. And it will not do for Christians simply to lament this: the Athenians of Paul's age did not take it for granted that any particular philosophy or religion should be the basis of their lives. Yet Paul made his winsome appeal for Christian faith in that place.

Perhaps most important, it will not do for Christians in our age to profess that we are open to persons of different cultures, but to continue practices of worship and church style that send a different message. Evangelical Christians have done some very creative work in recent decades in embracing a huge variety of cultures (including the use of non-Western languages) in Christian worship and in visible forms of church leadership. We need to be quite sure that when we proclaim Christ above all human cultures, our worship and church life are consistent with this claim.

We are called, then, to take the multicultural world in which we live as a divine gift. We are called to make our appeal for Christian faith in this context. This calls for us to be open-minded toward and genuinely interested in the people around us. It calls for us to be relentlessly and uncompromisingly true to Jesus Christ in our time and place.

QUESTIONS FOR DISCUSSION

1. In what ways do you see evidence of a multicultural society in the world in which you live from day to day?
2. Do you see evidence, in the world in which you live, of people's resistance to the notion of absolute or universal truths?
3. Do you think that attitudes toward absolute values have changed since the time of your parents? If you have

children, do you see changing attitudes toward absolute values on the part of your children?

4. List five things that you believe to be absolute or essential Christian beliefs.

5. List five things you would hold to be opinions traditionally taught or practiced by Christians, but which are not essential to Christian faith.

6. How does the life of your own congregation reflect the change to a multicultural society? In what way could your congregation express openness to people of different cultural traditions, while remaining true to the Christian message?

CHAPTER 2

Biblical Authority in a Relativist World

So then, brothers and sisters, stand firm and hold fast to the traditions that you were taught by us, either by word of mouth or by our letter. (2 Thessalonians 2:15)

Introduction

The previous study unit considered the challenges to historic Christian faith posed by a multicultural society. Now we consider how this cultural outlook affects the basis of Christian authority, **the Holy Scriptures.** The suspicion of claims to absolute truth in a relativist world challenges the historic Christian insistence on the final authority of the Bible. In a relativist world, why should people trust the Bible above all other authorities, as Christians have historically taught?

Historic Christian Teaching on Biblical Authority

We may begin by simply describing historic Christian attitudes toward biblical authority, especially as they developed from the time of the Protestant Reformation. **Before the Reformation,** Christians typically thought of the authority of the Bible and of later Christian traditions as being bound up together. God, they believed, had spoken both in the Scriptures and throughout the history of the Christian church. The saints of every age testified to the continuing presence of God in the world and in the church.

The **Protestant Reformation** challenged the connection between the Bible and later Christian traditions. Protestants tended to see tradition as a corrupting influence in the church, and they insisted that the Bible stands over the church as the only norm for reforming the church's life. This perspective was expressed eloquently in the first Homily of the Church of England, which urges Christians to "search for the well of life in the books of the New and Old Testament, and not run to the stinking puddles of men's traditions, devised by men's imagination, for our justification and salvation" (Homily 1, in John Leith, ed., *Creeds of the Churches*, p. 232). The Reformation principle *sola scriptura* ("by the scripture alone") did not rule out the appeal to tradition altogether, and it did not rule out the use of reason in interpreting the Scripture, but it gave the clear priority in determining matters of faith and life to the Bible.

Historic Protestant teaching on the authority of the Scriptures used four particular terms to describe the authoritative nature of the Bible: unity, clarity, sufficiency, and inerrancy (or infallibility). In speaking of the **unity** of the Bible, the Reformers meant that the Bible contains one consistent message about God's redemption of humankind, and each part of the Bible expresses this theme. This meant, as they understood it, that both Testaments serve as witnesses to Christ, and the Testaments do not contradict each other. The unity of the Bible was a crucial element in their understanding of biblical authority; without it, the Bible's authority would be diluted by competing or contradictory messages.

In speaking of the **clarity** of the Bible, the Reformers meant that the message of the Bible is clear enough that a careful, unprejudiced reading of it will tell what we need to know for our salvation and for the reform of the church. They generally insisted that the Bible must be studied with attention to the original languages (Hebrew, Aramaic, and Greek) in which it was written. They stressed that the Bible is its own best interpreter: more obscure passages of scripture must be interpreted in the light of clearer passages. This presupposes their confidence in the unity of the biblical message (as we have just seen). The clarity of the Bible was such that it did not require the judgment of later Christian teachers or traditions (as Catholics had insisted) to make its meaning clear.

In speaking of the **sufficiency** of the Bible, the Reformers mean that the Bible contains everything we need to know for our salvation and for the reform of the church. Again, this point presupposes the unity and clarity of the Bible. It is this point, however, that makes it most clear that later traditions, however illuminating or helpful they may be, are not necessary in the way that the Bible alone is necessary. Only the Scriptures offer a completely sufficient account of what humans need for salvation and for the life of the Christian church.

Catholics and Protestants in the Reformation age spoke of the **inerrancy** or **infallibility** of the Scriptures. Although the Church of England did not use these terms in its Articles of Religion, belief in scriptural inerrancy was widely shared during the Reformation. But in using the terms "inerrant" and "infallible," Protestant teachers meant that the Scriptures do not err or fail, particularly in what they teach about human salvation and the reform of the church. The Scriptures are completely reliable, because they immediately reflect God's own will. It may be important to note at this point that the Reformers' concern with inerrancy or infallibility had mainly to do with the Bible's reliability in matters of faith and Christian practice. As we shall see, the issue of the reliability of the Scriptures for matters of scientific truths or historical truths came to be disputed by the 1700s.

Challenges to Biblical Authority

These traditional Protestant understandings of biblical authority were challenged in the 1700s by the outlook of **the Enlightenment**. The Enlightenment brought a pervasive philosophical and scientific perspective that challenged all traditional authorities, including the authority of the Bible. If we want to know about the world, the Enlightenment suggested, it is best to rely on pure reason, or on our experience and observation of the world. Tradition might be wrong: Aristotle, for example, simply erred in claiming that spiders have six legs. He hadn't counted them (or, perhaps he only counted the legs of defective spiders). And the Bible might be wrong, especially in its

17

claims about the material universe and about history. The Enlightenment led to widespread questioning of the claims of the Bible grounded in **scientific investigation**, for example, in Charles Darwin's scientific account *The Origin of Species*. Thus the Creation account in Genesis could be relegated to obscurity.

The Enlightenment's challenges to biblical authority led to new forms of biblical scholarship in the 1800s, including the **historical-critical approach to the study of the Bible**. In particular, traditional belief in the unity of the Bible was challenged through the 1800s by evidence of multiple traditions that lay behind the biblical texts. The New Testament itself, many scholars came to believe, reflected the views of a variety of different communities. Matthew and Luke could be seen as the combination of a simple, earlier account of Jesus' acts (like the Gospel of Mark gives) with a different source that recorded Jesus' sayings or teachings. Books of the Old Testament could be thought of as compilations from a variety of different source traditions. Through the 1800s and 1900s, these critical studies of the Bible eroded the historic belief that a single, divine source lay behind the whole of the Jewish and Christian scriptures. In his study *The Eclipse of the Biblical Narrative*, Professor Hans Frei of Yale Divinity School has shown how the biblical story dropped out of Western consciousness as a central cultural motif in this period. We now live in a world that is, for the most part, biblically illiterate, and many people do not see a great deal of relevance in the Bible.

A multicultural society also poses a challenge to biblical authority. Its challenge is not that of a critical examination of the Scriptures. Rather, its challenge is posed to the whole notion of a single document that claims divine authority. Within the range of sacred scriptures of the world's religions, within the range of all the various grounds on which people make claims today, why should the Christian Bible have the first place of authority? And even if one grants that the Bible should have authority, why should we favor traditional Western understandings of the Bible over those from other cultures? At the beginning of the third Christian millennium, a number of cultural forces have come together to challenge the dominance of biblical authority.

The Wesleyan Contribution

The Wesleyan inheritance gives us some important insights for the recovery of a sense of biblical authority in our situation. In the first place, **the Wesleyan tradition has been clear about its commitment to the central authority of the Bible.** The United Methodist Confession of Faith and Articles of Religion make clear our commitment to the historic Protestant insistence on the unity, clarity and sufficiency of the Scriptures. Although they do not use the language of biblical inerrancy or infallibility, John Wesley affirmed these ideas, as they were understood in the time of the Protestant Reformation.

This commitment to the central place of biblical authority has not gone without challenges in churches of the Wesleyan tradition. A 1972 statement of the United Methodist Church on "Our Theological Task" described the manner in which United Methodists should consult the authority of scripture, tradition, reason, and experience as grounds for our beliefs and practices. In popular discussions, this came to be called the "Wesleyan Quadrilateral" (although the *Discipline* did not attribute it to John Wesley), and led to the impression that the authorities of tradition, experience, and reason might somehow have an equal or parallel authority with the Bible. Although the framers of the 1972 statement did not intend to leave the primacy of the Scripture in doubt, the language of the statement was the consistent subject of United Methodist discussions in the late 1970s and the 1980s.

In response to these concerns, the 1988 General Conference altered the language of the statement on "Our Theological Task" to make clear our commitment to the final authority of the Bible. "United Methodists share with other Christians the conviction that Scripture is the primary source and criterion for Christian doctrine," the revised statement reads, and "In theological reflection, the resources of tradition, experience, and reason are integral to our study of Scripture without displacing Scripture's primacy for faith and practice." In fact, the revised statement repeatedly affirms the primacy (or "first place") of the Holy Scriptures among the authorities of our faith and life.

A second contribution of the Wesleyan tradition in regard to biblical authority is that **the Wesleyan tradition has consistently affirmed a learned approach to scripture that affirms the fundamental unity of the Bible**. That is to say, our tradition has encouraged biblical learning and critical biblical scholarship, while insisting that the unity of the Bible remains fundamental to our faith. John Wesley himself used critical biblical studies available in his day (such as the annotations of German scholar Johann Albrecht Bengel). Wesley's colleague Adam Clarke produced a very learned *Commentary* on the whole Bible that became a staple of Methodist teachers throughout the 1800s. When other denominational traditions (especially Presbyterians and Baptists) were torn apart over issues of biblical inerrancy and infallibility, Methodists were not as severely affected. This was partly because Methodists had not traditionally used the terminology of inerrancy and infallibility, but also because the commitment to critical biblical scholarship had seldom been seriously challenged in Methodist circles.

A third contribution of the Wesleyan tradition has been **our commitment to read the Scriptures in the light of God's work in the past and in our own time**. Although Wesley himself did not have a conception of "tradition" as we use the term today (that is, the past that we value highly), he did appreciate and value the work of God in the ancient church, in the time of the Reformation, and even at points in the Middle Ages. Moreover, Wesley constantly read the Bible in the light of his own experience of God, and with the light afforded by reflection on the world around him. These two items would answer roughly to "experience" and "reason" as they are discussed in the statement of "Our Theological Task" in the United Methodist *Book of Discipline*. The point, however, was not to use "experience" and "reason" as abstract qualities or philosophical methods; Wesley's point was to recognize the presence of the divine mystery in our own lives and even in the broader world around us. Because the same God who inspired the Scriptures inspires us, because God's "eternal power and divine nature, invisible though they are, have been understood and seen through the things he has made" (Romans1:20), we can read the Bible faithfully in the light afforded by the divine presence today.

Conclusion

We need to ask ourselves, though, if we in fact own the authority of Scripture over our own lives and over the lives of our congregations. A practical test is to ask "Do you expect to be changed when you read the Bible?" If one does not really expect to be changed by reading the Bible, then for all our talk about biblical authority, we do not really own it. To own the authority of the Bible is to face the reality, every time we open it, that God will have a fresh, new message for us, one that may challenge us very deeply.

We can also ask if our ways of reading and even handling the Bible reflect our reverence for God's Word. Observe how Jews process with the Torah in a *shabat* (Sabbath) service, or how Eastern Orthodox Christians and Anglicans solemnly process with the Gospel book. Their very manners of handling the Bible express reverence. Too often we handle the Bible in the manner of a suburban telephone directory, and we read it aloud as if it had the authority of a newspaper editorial. Whatever we may say about the primacy of the Scriptures, such acts and such manners of reading betray our own lack of reverence for the divine word revealed in the Bible. A renewed commitment to biblical authority will bring a renewed sense of reverence for God's book, the precious gift that has been committed to the church.

As Wesleyan Christians living in a multicultural society, then, we bring this great gift of the Scriptures to our world. But the world outside of our churches is unlikely to perceive the depth and beauty of the biblical message if we ourselves do not handle the Scriptures reverently. Moreover, our own lives must serve as witnesses that we want to be a people normed or guided by the sacred Scriptures.

QUESTIONS FOR DISCUSSION

1. In your own experience, where do you see the challenges to the Bible posed by (a) critical modern scholarship, and (b) life in a multicultural society?
2. In what ways do you expect to be changed by reading the Bible?

3. Does your congregation's manner of handling the Bible and reading the Bible in church reflect reverence for the divine Scriptures?

4. How would you explain the importance of the Bible to someone unfamiliar with Christian beliefs?

CHAPTER 3

The Divine Trinity
in a Multicultural Age

*The grace of the Lord Jesus Christ, and the love of God, and
the communion of the Holy Spirit be with all of you.*
(2 Corinthians 13:13)

Introduction

Secularism challenges personal morality and the meaning of
life. The need for acceptance and tolerance apparent in a multicultural society also presents a spiritual challenge to Christians. How
do Christians take seriously the sovereignty of God, the redemption
and reconciling of the world through Jesus Christ, and the guiding
and sustaining power of the Holy Spirit? What sort of God do we
worship? The question is not new. The distinctively Christian doctrine of the Trinity was developed by the early church to answer
such a question. Wesleyan Christians have been consistent in teaching that the doctrine of the Trinity is foundational for Christians.
But explaining this doctrine was not and is not simple. In a multicultural society, we have to be very clear what the doctrine of the
Trinity does and does not mean.

The Concept of the Trinity

Where do you begin to describe the indescribable? Though the
concept of the Trinity cannot be inexhaustibly explained or com-

23

prehended, it does help us to know about God. The doctrine of the Trinity does not try to explain the existence of God or what God's "substance" might be, but it does set some practical limits on the teaching about God. It is a distinctive Christian concept, an essential teaching of Christian belief and formative for faith. Opposition or misunderstanding occurs because "Trinity" is not a biblical word, and some claim that the doctrine conflicts with monotheism, the belief in one God as taught by the Bible. John Wesley declined to explain the Trinity, and in sermons and letters commented: "Tell me how it is that in this room there are three candles and but one light, and I will explain to you the [Trinity]."

Essential for Christian Belief and Worship

The doctrine of the Trinity is essential for Christian belief to avoid falling into error in our thinking about God, and our worship of this God. The biblical imperative is that there is one God and we are to worship no other god. "Jesus answered, 'It is written, 'Worship the Lord your God, and serve only him'" (Luke 4:8). In ancient times people made "graven images" of God, and these human constructions are condemned in the Hebrew Scriptures. Our concern today is not so much the danger of *metal* images, but danger of the *mental* images that we may construct on our own about God. In fact, John Wesley warned that the "gravest" idol is false religion, which might even be a kind of outward or nominal religious orthodoxy, but lacking in transforming power.

What must be explained is that the eternal God has always existed as Father, Son, and Holy Spirit. There are many helpful scriptural images and metaphors for God. The Bible gives insight into the kind of God we worship through the relational words Father, Son, and Holy Spirit. God is referred to as "Father," "the Father of all Comfort," "the Everlasting Father," "the Son of God," "the Word," the "Spirit of God," "the Spirit of Christ," "the Advocate," and "the Spirit of Truth" to name a few. These images help us to better know the infinite God. The doctrine of the Trinity helps us to understand God, while at the same time limiting an attempt to create God out of our own imagination. That is to say, the teaching about the divine Trinity is a way of keeping our teaching about God in keeping with the biblical revelation that God has made.

A newspaper article discussed people who were building their own unique religion, salvaging what they liked from the Bible and discarding the rest. The article went on to say that the God of the Old Testament who was vengeful and angry was discarded, but Jesus was kept because he was likable and big on love. People are constantly re-creating God. If a traditional doctrine conflicts with their lifestyle, they may select another doctrine (perhaps another church) and adjust the concept of God rather than alter their lifestyle. Historic Christian teaching about the sacred Trinity does not allow us this kind of consumer-oriented selection of gods. The doctrine of the Trinity tells of the God revealed in the Scripture through Jesus Christ, active in the world through the Holy Spirit.

What Makes the Doctrine of the Trinity Necessary?

Hear, O Israel: the Lord our God, the Lord is one. (Mark 12:29)

In a multicultural society, Christianity is confronted with a multiplicity of gods. Judaism and Islam have long suspected that Christianity itself worships more than one God. The biblical narrative is clear in affirming that we are to worship one God alone. How do we answer the concern that trinitarianism is just another form of polytheism (i.e., belief in many gods)? We need to be clear about the fact that historic Christianity is monotheistic. We believe in one God, Judaism's God, the God revealed in the Old and New Testaments. Christian faith is devotion and obedience to a single God.

What distinguishes the way Christian theology looks at the frame of reference of God? It is focused on Christ and how God is revealed through Jesus. A proper understanding of the Trinity does not overemphasize the work of Christ, or of any one Person of the Trinity, while minimizing the others. The doctrine of the Trinity teaches the wholeness of the Father, Son, and Holy Spirit working together, and never a separateness of trinitarian activity. The Trinity is the absolute epitome of social interaction and unity.

When we look at Jesus we learn something about God. God enters into solidarity with humanity, and enters into suffering with the lost. The church has maintained that the incarnation (God's coming "in the flesh" in Christ) demands an explanation that can only be articulated in trinitarian language. To tell the gospel story correctly, it is essential to appeal to the God of Abraham, Isaac, and Jacob, who is revealed through the incarnation, death, and resurrection of Jesus Christ, and actively present in the world by the power of the Holy Spirit. Communion with God and solidarity with broken and suffering humanity are joined in Jesus' coming into the world.

The primary purpose of the doctrine of the Trinity is to explain the gospel message. The doctrine results from the attempt to be faithful to the biblical narrative and God's self-disclosure to humanity. It is not speculative theology. In the Bible, God is revealed in the three distinct and divine Persons of the Father, Son, and Holy Spirit. John Wesley's favored expression was the "three-one God." The traditional thinking and imagery of God, as a triune God, is necessary in light of God's divine, saving activity through the incarnation of Jesus Christ, and through the continuing active presence of the Holy Spirit. The disclosure of God in this "Christ-event" informs us that the God of the Old Testament is the God of the New Testament. Through the doctrine of the Trinity the church attempts to clarify how Christ relates to God, and how this God is experienced in present, living relationship through the Holy Spirit.

The Historic Development

Let us first consider the historic development of the doctrine of the Trinity. The need for the doctrine was precipitated by arguments whether Christ was a created being, or deity. These arguments were not theoretical; they grew out of the church's central practice of the worship of Jesus Christ. The question arose whether or not it was appropriate to worship Christ as God. The words associated with the doctrine of the Trinity are attributed to the ancient African Christian convert, Tertullian, who first used the Latin word *trinitas* and the associated words *persona* and *substantia,* in his discussions about God. These words describe a Being who speaks and acts, relates to others, and exists in a social relationship. The contemporary understanding of "person" adds further confusion. *Persona* did not necessarily mean persons as separate individual beings, but the God of one substance who is revealed in a distinct threefold role as Father, Son, and Holy Spirit. "Substance" (*substantia*) is that essential being of God, common to all three Persons of the Godhead. It is unity and oneness, while maintaining a differentiation of the Persons. We can even say that we do not rightly or fully know what the "substance" of God actually is; we use the term as a way of speaking of that which is common to the Father, the Son, and the Holy Spirit.

Personhood and communion are central elements of Christian belief. God is spoken about in personal terms such as love, anger, purpose, and will. However, this speaking of God in human terms is not to equate God with human limitation, but to indicate the divine ability and willingness to relate to others. Person as a distinction in the Godhead is not representative of the whole person in the human sense. In human persons we tend to think of an individual self-consciousness and self-sufficiency. For the Trinity, the implication is not three centers of consciousness, but a shared consciousness. The Godhead is united in all divine activity. There are scriptures that interchange the roles of the Father as creator with Jesus, and scriptures that refer to the Holy Spirit as the Spirit of Christ (John 1:1-2; Romans 8:9-11; Ephesians 3:16-19). The Persons of the Godhead are differentiated but undivided and interpenetrating.

The Controversies

The Arian controversy in the 300s A.D. involved the claim that though Christ was divine in some sense, he was nonetheless a "created being." This is a contemporary issue in multiculturalism. What is at stake is whether or not Christ is "the one and only way to the Father," or just one of the ways. The finality and exclusivity of Christ will be discussed in a later chapter in this study. The Arian teachers denied that Christ was coequal and coeternal with the uncreated Father, and therefore, was not to be worshiped in the same manner as the Father. Jesus Christ and the Holy Spirit were not God, but highly exalted "creatures" (that is, created beings).

The heart of the matter is simply whether or not Christ is to be worshiped as God. The Nicene Creed is the response of councils of Christian bishops in A.D. 325 and A.D. 381 to this Arian debate. It refutes the claim that Christ is a created being, and clarifies that Christ is "of one substance with the Father, begotten, not created," and that the Holy Spirit is "together worshipped and glorified" with the Father and Son. The councils did not in fact use the word "Trinity" to define the concept that the Father, Son, and Holy Spirit are eternally and equally God. The Arian controversy was settled by the consensus that the Father and Son were "of one being."

Though chronologically earlier, the Sabellian Controversy centered on the issue of the eternal and simultaneous existence of the three Persons of the Godhead. Sabellius argued that there is only one God, and he insisted that God is only one Person. Further, he maintained that God has appeared in three successive roles in human history. The one eternal person reveals himself on different occasions in three roles of God as Father, Son, and Holy Spirit. This heresy is defined as "modalism," which denies that Christ and the Holy Spirit are distinct Persons sharing the one nature of God the Father. The fallacy of this position is that there are several scriptural references to the entire Godhead (Father, Son, and Holy Spirit) and these references cannot be reduced simply to functions or roles. As previously mentioned the Father, Son, and Holy Spirit are all three present at the same time. The Trinity is present at the baptism of Jesus. God the Father speaks from heaven concerning His beloved Son, and the Holy Spirit descends on Jesus in the visible form of a dove (Mark 1:9-11).

Jesus also evokes a Three-One God in the baptismal formula of the Great Commission given in Matthew 28: " Go therefore and make disciples of all nations, baptizing them in the name of the

Father and of the Son and of the Holy Spirit, and teaching them to obey everything that I have commanded you" (Matthew 28:19-20). The doctrine of the Trinity emphasizes the oneness of God without disregarding the distinct Persons of the Godhead who are always together and always cooperating.

The Old Testament God Is the New Testament God

The doctrine of the Trinity connects us to the Old Testament through Jesus Christ, and the God that Jesus calls "Father." In the Old Testament no explicit examples of the Three-One God exist; however, there are vague references that contain indications of the plurality of God as later revealed in the New Testament as the One God revealed in Three Persons. Examples of these implicit, plural forms include the name for God, Elohim, which is plural, and references to God that are certainly plural ("Then God said, 'Let us make humankind in our image, according to our likeness...'" Genesis 1:26), and numerous references to the Holy Spirit, Spirit of the Lord, and Spirit of God (see Genesis 1:2; Psalm 33:6; and Isaiah 40:17).

It is also possible to see the relationship of God and Jesus Christ creating, sustaining, and accomplishing "all things" through the spoken word of God, where "word" implies more than power (for example Psalms 33:6, 148:5-6; Isaiah 40:8). Further, it is possible to connect the Trinity of the New Testament with the implication that the God of the Old Testament is disclosed in three distinct ways: that is, God and the Spirit of God (Genesis 1:2), the word [Word] of the Lord, the breath [Spirit] (Psalm 33:6), to cite a few. We find the word of God attributed to Christ, the "Word," in John's Gospel (John 1:1ff), and that the world was made through him. Christ's participation in creation is affirmed where Paul states that, "in him [Christ] all things in heaven and on earth were created" (Colossians 1:16). All these references find fulfillment in the New Testament that proclaims Jesus as the Word that creates, and that reveal Jesus as the full image (expression) of the invisible God (Colossians 1:15-19).

Generally what we understand as the God revealed in the Old Testament is the God referred to by the name "Father" in the New

Testament. The Person of the Father is understood to be the uncreated (or "unoriginated") God. The conceptual language of "Father" is linked to the biblical notion of God the Son, and illustrates that the Trinity, the Three-One God, lives in a relational community of persons.

To hold a trinitarian view of God is to see God, the Father, actively involved in the redeeming and reconciling of the world through the atonement of the Son and the active grace of the Holy Spirit. He redeems and reconciles the world through the incarnation, life, death, and resurrection of Jesus Christ, and through the active presence of the Holy Spirit who continues to complete God's salvation of believers by empowering and transforming grace to partake of the life of Christ.

God's fatherhood expresses a special relationship. The fatherhood of God is not to be simply equated with the human concept of fatherhood and having children. The term "Father" reflects relational language and indicates that God lives in loving relationship and communion. Though there are Old Testament Scriptures that employ the imagery of God as a Father, and God as the Father of Israel (child), there are no prayers that are addressed to God as Father, indicating the intimate relationship of God as our "Father" that is revealed to us through Jesus Christ. Christ, as the Son, further reveals this God we know as Father. We are invited to address God as "our Father" in prayer and also are able to consider ourselves to be the children of God (Matthew 6:9-18; John 1:12; Romans 8:14).

Again, though there are several references to the Holy Spirit or Spirit of God in the Old Testament (for example, Exodus 31:3; Psalm 51:11; Isaiah 11:2 and 63:11), it becomes apparent that with the incarnation of Jesus and the New Testament references to the Holy Spirit and distinctions about the Holy Spirit as divine and equal with the Father, the doctrine of the Trinity was necessary to explain this Three-One God who is the God of the Old Testament.

The Trinity and the Incarnation

The doctrine of the Trinity in its most simple application explains the incarnation, the human meaning of Jesus. Jesus was conceived by the Holy Spirit and born of the Virgin Mary. E. Stanley Jones always reminded believers that we do not believe in Jesus because of the Virgin Birth; we believe in the Virgin Birth because of Jesus. The Virgin Birth is not necessary because it protects Jesus from the contamination of original sin, but to convey God's intentional intervention into human history. Original sin is the human condition of alienation from God and the propensity to sin, which is common to all humanity. We will deal with this problem of the universal sinfulness of humanity in the next chapter.

Jesus was not just another human being, but God becoming human. "For in him the whole fullness of deity dwells bodily" (Colossians 2:9). In becoming human Christ did not stop being God. The doctrine of the Trinity made it clear that Christ was "of one being" with the Father. However, it was important for the Christian community to declare that Christ was fully human. Jesus entered into solidarity with suffering humanity, experiencing life and death as a human. In Christ the human and divine were perfectly united. The Council of Chalcedon in A.D. 451 arrived at the consensus that "two natures" (divine and human) were united in the "one Person" of Christ. Methodists and others in the Wesleyan tradition include the dual nature of Christ in their Articles of Religion.

A college professor stated: "Jesus was God letting us watch him live." Jesus confirms this when he declares, "The Father and I are one" (John 10:30). Later in the Gospel of John, Philip asked Jesus to show the disciples the Father and Jesus answered, "Have I been with you all this time, Philip, and you still do not know me? Whoever has seen me has seen the Father. How can you say, 'Show us the Father'?" (John 14: 9).

Another example is Thomas's response to the invitation to touch the hands and side of the resurrected Christ with: "My Lord and My God!" (John 20:28).

The Nicene Creed was revised in A.D. 381 to clarify how the Holy Spirit relates to the Father and the Son. The Son originates (is

31

begotten) from the Father. The Son is coeternal and coequal with the Father. The Holy Spirit originates from ("proceeds from") the Father. Is the Spirit coequal and coeternal with the Father and Son, and to be worshiped as God? The Creed makes it clear that the Holy Spirit is God and is to be accorded equal reverence with the Father and the Son. A later adaptation of the Creed states the Holy Spirit proceeds from the Father *and the Son*.

The Holy Spirit is the actualization of God's presence in the life and experience of the believer. The Holy Spirit is the active grace of God, guiding and sustaining us in the "way of salvation" that we will talk about in later chapters of this study. This stress on the present activity of the Holy Spirit not only characterized historic Methodist piety, but also flowed from Methodism into the Holiness and Pentecostal movements. Salvation is the work of all the Persons of the Trinity, and the mystery of God is such that we cannot divide out the works of God.

Augustine commenting on the two greatest commandments, loving God and loving others, verifies the early church's understanding of the Holy Spirit as God. "And no one fulfills this law but he who receives the gift, the Holy Spirit, who is, in very truth, equal to the Father and the Son; for the Trinity itself is God, and in this God must all our hope be placed" (*Ancient Christian Writers,* No. 2, ed. by Johannes Quasten and Joseph C. Plumpe (New York: Newman Press, 1946), p. 87.) The Persons of the Godhead cannot be reduced to functions. In the work of salvation each of the three Persons of the Godhead works together on our behalf (compare Romans 8:12-17).

Emphasizing the radical and intensely *personal* nature of God is the historical and distinctive teaching of Methodists and Wesleyans about God. What Methodist and Wesleyan evangelical doctrine teaches about the worship of the Trinity, the nature of Christ, and the Holy Spirit is consonant with the faith of the historic Christian community. Our teaching about God grows out of our worship, where we name the true subject of our adoration: "Glory be to the Father, and to the Son, and to the Holy Spirit."

Gender-Specific Language About God

Are we obligated to use the language of the Council of Bishops of A.D. 325 and A.D. 381? Must God be addressed exclusively in masculine terms? To address God as Father and Jesus as Son is not to imply that God is male. The first Article of Religion states that God is "without body or parts." God is without gender; God is spirit. Other language, nouns and pronouns, can serve as descriptive tools that enhance the traditional language, revealing and representing the "three-one God" as three distinct but undivided Persons. New language and alternative expressions must be careful not to diminish the coequality or relational aspects of each Person of the Godhead.

It is important to dismantle the implications of language often used to validate sexism, domination, and oppression. Misinterpretation and misappropriation of patriarchal formulas, which intend to emphasize relational equality and the self-giving love of personhood, have brutalized and victimized women and children. However, there has not yet developed a consensus or agreement in the Christian communities in finding new language about God, for example, whether we should use the word "Mother" in referring to the first Person of the Trinity in the same manner in which we have used the word "Father" in the past.

"Father," "Son," and "Holy Spirit" are words that depict a shared, self-giving love relationship. God is not an aloof authority figure who delights in subjugating others. God desires to be in loving, personal relationship with humanity, male and female. Male and female are created in the image of this personal God. God is neither male nor female and transcends the human distinctions between the genders. The traditional language insists on helping the believer unpack how real personhood is defined and revealed in relationship. The mystery of God cannot be fully described by a single metaphor or image. If God is not stereotyped to be male, it is conceivable and appropriate to use many images to describe God.

Conclusion

The doctrine of the Trinity is not a distinctly Methodist teaching. Rather, it is part of the inheritance of doctrine that Methodists have from the ancient Christian church. It developed out of an attempt to make sense of Christian worship in the ancient, multicultural society of the Roman world. It still expresses the distinct essence of ecumenical Christian faith, and needs to be explained clearly in the multicultural world in which we live today. In this teaching, Wesleyan Christians join the chorus of the worldwide Christian community; indeed, we join with the saints of all ages, and "with angels and archangels and all the company of heaven," as we sing "Glory be to the Father, and to the Son, and to the Holy Spirit." Amen.

QUESTIONS FOR DISCUSSION

1. Why is the doctrine of the Trinity integral to the Christian communities' worship of God?
2. How is trinitarianism distinct from polytheism?
3. How is the concept of the Trinity demonstrated in the Bible?
4. Is the Arian controversy relevant in our postmodern and pluralistic world?
5. Are there other names that could be used to describe the Three-One God? Would these other names or designations convey the essential unity and yet the distinct differences? Do the terms imply relationship and community?

CHAPTER 4

Is Jesus *the* Only Way to God?

I am the way, and the truth, and the life. No one comes to the Father except through me. (John 14:6)

Introduction

One of the current debates in evangelical theology has to do with **religious pluralism,** and the relationship of Christianity to other great living religious traditions. Large-scale migrations have placed actual congregations of believers from the great religious traditions in close proximity to each other. In the course of a normal day we encounter a variety of cultural traditions. The deli worker at the supermarket may well be Hindu, the cashier Muslim, and the manager a practitioner of traditional African religion. In the corporate offices of business, medicine, law, and the hallways of schools we interact daily with the cultural and religious diversity of the world. It is easily observable that these people live full, productive, and wholesome lives apart from any Christian context or reference.

What does it mean to live as a Christian in communities that are becoming more non-Christian and in communities of more religious plurality? The earliest Christian confession of faith was *"Jesus is Lord"* (1 Corinthians 12:3). In a multicultural society it is often considered the height of arrogance to maintain an exclusive confession of faith that Jesus is Savior and Lord, and the only way to God.

35

What does it mean to profess Jesus Christ as Lord? There are numerous texts that seem to indicate that Jesus is the only way of salvation, and that Jesus is Lord. Further, that believing in him and calling upon his name brings salvation, and that at the name of Jesus every person will bow and confess Jesus Christ is Lord (for example, John 14:6; Acts 16:31; Romans 10:9-12; Philippians 2:10-11).

What does this mean about the salvation of non-Christians and those of other faiths? Are they going to hell because they do not believe in Jesus Christ as the Messiah, the Son of God? Since the proclaiming of the gospel has always taken place in a culturally and religiously pluralistic world, this is not a new challenge. However, the reality of today's multicultural society makes it a more insistent and immediate question.

The Finality of Christ

The central conviction of Christianity is that God and God's redemptive purpose for all of humanity is definitively revealed in Jesus Christ. This is commonly referred to as the ***Scandal of Particularity***. The unconditional, ultimate commitment to Jesus Christ as the unique and definitive, saving presence of God in human life is sometimes expressed as our belief in the ***finality of Christ***. Scriptural authority, conversion, and new life are the basic tenets of Wesleyan evangelicalism that are essential in articulating the doctrine of the finality of Christ.

Obviously, a position taken on religious pluralism and the **finality of Christ** can shape views about revelation, incarnation, the authority of the Scriptures, and the nature of the church. If **Jesus is Lord**, the implication is that there are some absolute truths that must shape and guide our lives. Beliefs about these matters in turn shape the practices of worship, education, evangelism, spiritual formation, and mission. If there are other means through which we can be saved, then why is it necessary to evangelize, preach or baptize in the name of Jesus?

In Matthew 16, Jesus makes it clear that it matters how we

respond to the question, **Who do we believe Jesus to be?** The disciples are first asked who people believe Jesus to be, and then asked for their response to that same question. **To confess that Jesus is Lord is to make an exclusive claim that other religions do not.**

Wesleyan Christians proclaim the sovereignty of Christ as the Savior and Lord of the world in a world where less than 34 percent of the world's population considers itself to be Christian. To maintain that Jesus is Lord is to imply that we are to live under Christ's rule and no area of life is outside of his control. It is important to remember that when Jesus asked, "Who do people say that I am?" the followers of Christ were a minority amid Judaism and the varied religious traditions of the ancient world.

Cultural and Religious Pluralism

Can Christians continue to affirm the *finality of Christ* in a world where the plurality of culture and religion increasingly point to the need for a spirit of openness and dialogue? Postmodern culture, disillusioned with traditionalism and modernism, highly values tolerance and diversity. It often suggests that all truth is relative to the individual. This view can lead to the conclusion that disagreement is intolerance and that all cultural values are equally valid, and equally to be approved.

The direct contradictions in cultural perspectives and values that marginalize, victimize, and oppress others makes this an untenable position. The dignity and worth of all human beings, male, female, and children cannot be compromised for the sake of political expediency or religious tolerance. **There are serious theological reasons for affirming cultural pluralism, but there are equally important theological reasons for making value judgments about particular patterns and practices of both cultural and religious pluralism.**

Affirming the doctrine of the **finality of Christ** requires clearly communicating it while still supporting the rights of others to disagree with our viewpoint. Pluralism does not necessarily breed relativism that dilutes and compromises the strength of the Christian witness.

37

Pluralism and ethical relativism at the very least demand the inviolability of human dignity. Tolerance does not mean equal validation of truth claims, and disagreement of core beliefs does not mean intolerance. Tolerance is not enough—you can tolerate without loving, but you cannot love without tolerating. Methodists and the Wesleyan tradition as a whole must be careful not to confuse truth with tolerance.

Wesleyan Christians must help people ask the right questions; contemporary apologetics must be more than combative and defensive. The doctrine of the **finality of Christ** does not legitimize violence and persecution in the name of Christ. The Bible teaches much more than just toleration for others, it teaches respect and love. It teaches the right to live a livable life.

Christians are convinced by experience that Christ offers the livable life, a life of holiness and happiness. John 10:10 verifies that Christ has come that those who believe might have a more abundant life, a life worth living. **It is the task of Christians to live and offer to others the livable life through Jesus Christ.**

The biblical warrant as we encounter people of other faiths is that we are all beloved children of God, and further, that God through Christ came to us; we did not come to God.

The claim of the **finality of Christ** is judged by the living out of the gospel message by those who profess to be Christians. Our lives must substantiate the reality of a relationship with Jesus Christ that alters and transforms our living. The **finality of Christ** is refuted and unpersuasive because there is so little of Jesus in the lives of those claiming to be Christians.

Isn't it narrow-minded for Christians to think that they are right and everyone else is wrong? A tenable theological position and a faith affirmation of the **finality of Jesus** as God Incarnate, the unique Savior of all humanity is possible. Our purpose is not to condemn other religions, to disprove or exclude the beliefs of others, but to live out the truth of Christianity. While it is not necessary to denigrate values found in other religious traditions, evangelicals must hold to the biblical belief in the **finality of Christ.**

It is not necessary for unity to accept all the implications and

38

imperatives of pluralism. A common argument for religious pluralism and religious tolerance is that all religions basically teach the same things. All are pathways to God and means of salvation, but use different names for God. As long as each person is genuinely sincere, what difference does it make what they believe? The problem is that sincerely believing something doesn't make it true. What counts is not just the sincerity of our faith, but also the *object* of our faith. One can be sincere, and sincerely wrong.

Strongly holding to particular beliefs about God doesn't make them true. It is possible to find the saving work of God operative in every religion without falling prey to the danger of syncretism. Syncretism is the indiscriminate adaption and combining of differing doctrines and beliefs (see chapter 1). Acknowledging the saving work of God outside of Christian churches or even outside of Christian cultures does not mean that there is a "way or path of salvation" outside of Jesus Christ.

Can we preach the gospel without preaching the incarnation, life, and death of Jesus, and the finality of Christ? E. Stanley Jones stated that the unique thing about Christianity is Christ, and not this idea or that idea about Christ. So all religions are not the same.

The incarnation at the least establishes a new historical reality and divine intention. To forfeit the uniqueness of Christ is to cease to be Christian. The Wesleyan tradition holds that Jesus Christ is not just another option among all the other religious faiths or cultural expressions, but the full revelation of God's plan of redemption for the world.

The texts cited earlier about the lordship and the **finality of Christ**, do not provide excuses or validation for "Christian" persecution of other faiths. Followers of Christ are to live in such a way that their lives show Christianity to be trustworthy. Respect for the equality and worth of all peoples is a value of universal importance in declaring a God who loves and desires to save the whole world.

The Wesleyan doctrine of universal atonement in Christ does not necessitate universalism—the doctrine that *all* will be saved.

Scripture is replete with references to the final condition of those who reject Christ. The universal accessibility of salvation does not disregard the biblical pronouncement of judgment and the possibility of rejection.

Though the Bible details God's final triumph over sin and evil, it promises no universal redemption. The final picture is always one of division—the wheat from the tares, the sheep from the goats—those on the inside of the door and those on the outside of the door. The language of casting out is always prevalent in eschatological talk and thought.

The Cosmic Christ

The universal implications of the **finality of Christ** is that Jesus died for all. God sent his Son to save the world; and when we confess the finality of Christ, we are confessing Jesus as the universal Savior. To hold this belief is not a narrow perspective. The Bible proclaims that the saved will come from all the corners of the earth.

After this I looked, and there was a great multitude that no one could count, from every nation, from all tribes and peoples and languages, standing before the throne and before the Lamb, robed in white, with palm branches in their hands. They cried out in a loud voice, saying,

"Salvation belongs to our God
who is seated on the
throne, and to the Lamb!" (Revelation 7:9-10)

Do all religious traditions and saving structures point to or lead to the *Cosmic Christ*? The notion of the *Cosmic Christ* is an understanding of the second Person of the Trinity that exists beyond the particularity of the historical Jesus of Nazareth. In some contemporary theology, it may mean the idea that it is through the Cosmic Christ that all paths of salvation are mediated. John 1:9 does make reference to the "true light," that "which enlightens everyone, was coming into the world," and the word for "world" here is *kosmos*. This is the biblical basis of the idea of the Cosmic

Christ. "The true light that gives light to every [person] was coming into the world [*kosmos*]." Wesley ascribed this verse to the working of prevenient grace, and the awakening of the need for salvation. **It is perfectly consistent to hold that Jesus is the exclusive way to God, and to claim that people can encounter God outside Christianity, without knowing about the historical Jesus of Nazareth.** Wherever we encounter good and a sincere seeking for God, we can attribute it to the prevenient grace of God active through the Holy Spirit operative in the life of every person whether Christian or not. Nonetheless, prevenient grace is not justifying grace, and Wesley was clear that those who reject Jesus Christ will be lost.

Three Theological Positions:
Exclusivism, Inclusivism, and Pluralism

A reexamination of the uniqueness and **finality of Christ** has resulted from this shifting paradigm of cultural and religious pluralism. The three major theological positions and commonly discussed views have been described as exclusivism, inclusivism, and pluralism.

The exclusivist view contends that Christianity alone holds the truth, and that all other religions and faith commitments are false. This assertion maintains a narrow salvation exclusively through Christ. Further, it holds that general or natural revelation can enlighten, but cannot enable salvation. For the most part this view requires a conversion experience, a real transformation. This view holds that even the unevangelized are lost. While this concept may fit the doctrine of predestination and election, it does not square with doctrine of the universal availability of grace, especially the view of prevenient grace held by Wesleyan Christians.

The inclusivist view maintains that salvation comes through Christ, but is not limited to the historical event of the incarnation: life, death, and resurrection of Christ. Included in the concept are those who at death find that Christ is the source of their salvation through the mercy of God. For the unevangelized (those

41

who have not heard the message about Christ) this means living faithfully to all the light that has been revealed to them and trusting in the mercy of God. However, Christians who take the inclusivist view usually do maintain that the atoning grace made explicit in Jesus remains the normative way of salvation.

Finally, the pluralist view holds that God is at work in all religions and that they are agencies of salvation. On this view, it is not necessary to have a personal relationship with or even acknowledge Jesus Christ as Savior and Lord. This point of view typically holds that all paths lead to God. This is universalism at its height.

The Finality of Christ: Jesus Is Lord

All religions make ultimate or absolute claims at some point, and Christians ought to make such a claim in the matter of the *finality of Jesus Christ*. The central belief that Jesus is Lord is an exclusivity that cannot be given up. John Wesley opposed any trend leading to an uncritical pluralism. Wesley's frequently quoted dictum of "If thy heart is right as my heart is right, give me thy hand," affords a "catholic spirit" only in matters that are nonessential (see chapter 1). In the same sermon on a "Catholic Spirit," Wesley insisted that there are "essential doctrines" that cannot be compromised or negotiated because they are foundational for Christian faith.

From the beginning Christians have proclaimed that the only way of salvation, the only way to God, is through Jesus Christ. The exclusive message of Paul in Romans 10:9-13 is that confessing Jesus as Lord and trusting in Him brings salvation: **"Because if you confess with your lips that Jesus is Lord and believe in your heart that God raised him from the dead, you will be saved."** To confess Jesus Christ as Lord is to deny that any other is Lord.

Wesley emphasized the centrality of personal faith in Christ, and contended that it was essential that Christ be offered to everyone. The uniqueness of Jesus is not a narrow exclusivity, but by its very proclamation it is a theological mandate for inclusivity. It is the very nature of incarnation that barriers are broken down or crossed so that the universality of the gospel becomes operative in the given context and moment.

Wesleyan theology must negotiate between the extremes of exclusivism and relativism. Is God only disclosed through Christ? Some scriptural passages, such as John 14:6, appear to make such a claim: "I am the way, and the truth, and the life. No one comes to the Father except through me." **Will those who never encounter the gospel of Christ be lost?** If it is God's will that all should be saved (2 Peter 3:9), how do Wesleyan Christians correlate this with the demands that a theological position of the **finality of Christ** makes?

Because God's grace cooperates with human beings and God holds persons accountable for their responses, Wesley found it difficult to align the knowledge of a merciful God with the condemnation and rejection of those who had no opportunity to respond to the gospel. **He allowed room that God could save apart from explicit faith in Jesus Christ. The scripture informs us that God's general revelation can bring people to knowledge of God: Romans 1 and 2 provide this possibility.**

Those who have no opportunity to hear the gospel are compelled to "walk in all the light that they have," and they will be judged according to that light. This general revelation and acknowledgment of God is the work of the Holy Spirit and the benefit of the atoning work of Christ. Wesley concluded that it is our task and responsibility to preach and present the gospel to every person. If there really is a God like the Bible describes and that God works through the Holy Spirit in the lives of all persons, then our responsibility is to tell the story with the expectation that God is working. What will be revealed, however, will not contradict that which is known about and through Christ.

The New Testament story of Jesus is normative, and to deny the uniqueness and the incarnation of Jesus is to forfeit the authority of the Scripture. Wesleyan Christians take the Bible seriously and locate their own personal story within the context of the biblical story. Though Wesleyans may not use the language of

43

inerrancy, we do not deny that every scripture is inspired by God (see chapter 2). We believe the Scriptures contain all truth necessary to reveal the redemptive purposes of God in Christ for humanity (and for the life of the church). Thus while commitment to Jesus as the definitive expression of God's character and purpose belongs to the nonnegotiable core of Christian faith, Christians also humbly acknowledge that they are far from comprehending the mystery of God in Christ.

The Necessity of Conversion

In Wesleyan theology there exists a high priority on conversion. **The question is not so much of a dramatic conversion or even a crisis moment, but whether or not there has been a real change in the person.** The appropriation of God's grace results in a real transformation. Through grace we are empowered by the Holy Spirit to become Christlike.

The test of knowing Christ is whether or not we obey him. Jesus stated, "He who has My commandments and keeps them, he it is who loves Me . . . ?" (John 14:21 NASB). This obedience, however, is not to some legalistically imposed standard, but an obedience that springs from loving abandonment to Christ in one's heart. Alister McGrath stipulates that it is not the memory or experience of past conversion that is important. What is fundamentally important is present convertedness. In Wesley's terms, do we love God with all our hearts, minds, and strength and our neighbor as ourselves?

Conclusion—A Wesleyan View

Following the example of Lesslie Newbigin, it is possible to formulate a tenable **Wesleyan evangelical position on the finality of Christ**. First, it is **exclusive** in affirming the uniqueness of Christ and confesses him as Savior of the world. Second, it is **inclusive** in the sense that the saving grace of God is not limited, and denies that only those who have had the opportunity to hear the gospel will be saved. However, it rejects the notion that non-Christian religions are means or ways of salvation. Finally, it is **pluralistic** in recognizing the active presence and working of prevenient grace in the lives of all human beings, although it rejects any formula or way of salvation that denies the atoning work of God through the particularity of Jesus Christ of Nazareth, as the Son of the Living God.

Returning to the confessional statement that **Jesus is Lord**, this affirmation of Jesus constrains us to ask ourselves, more importantly, **who do we say that Jesus Christ is?** The ultimate fate of others who do not believe in Jesus is left in the hands of a loving and righteous God. Our concern is what our lives say about Christ as we relate to others and the world around us. Do our lives demonstrate the reality that Jesus is the Savior and Lord of the world? **Our purpose is not to prove other religions wrong, but to live as though Christianity is true.** That is one of the supreme, practical challenges of living as a contemporary Wesleyan Christian in a multicultural society.

QUESTIONS FOR DISCUSSION

1. What are some specific instances in which it is possible to separate tolerance and the validation of truth claims?
2. What are some ways of guiding others to "ask the right questions"?
3. How would you compare and contrast the three major theological positions toward religious pluralism?
4. What is the distinction between general and specific revelation?

CHAPTER 5

The Holy Spirit and the Spirit of the Age

Now we have received not the spirit of the world, but the Spirit that is from God, so that we may understand the gifts bestowed on us by God. (1 Corinthians 2:12)

Introduction

In the second chapter, we considered the example of Paul on Mars Hill (Acts 17), and the way in which he explained the gospel to the Athenians by referring to their own religious shrines and their own poets. For a long time, Christians felt that Paul's challenge was irrelevant for modern people. Modern culture, they thought, had become so secular that it would not make sense to appeal to religious traditions as a beginning point to explain the Christian faith. But the situation has changed immensely in a multicultural society where we are again confronted with the challenge of explaining the Christian faith in a context of multiple, competing religious traditions.

Perhaps the modern world was never really as secular as some interpreters held it to be. Studies undertaken by the Religious Experience Institute at Manchester College, Oxford, in the 1970s showed that a large percentage of British people—a majority, in fact—claimed to have identifiably religious experiences, and this despite the fact that attendance at traditional religious services in Britain amounted to perhaps 5 percent of the overall population. Similar studies in the United States conducted by the Gallup organization show quite similar results with respect to the frequency with which people reported having religious experiences. Since the 1970s, these figures have in fact gone higher. Interest in spirituality has perhaps never been higher than at the present time.

This means that, despite all of the talk about secularization in modern life, **we live in a time when men and women are in fact quite keenly interested in religion**. They're just not as interested in institutional religious life. Here we are, then, on Mars Hill with Paul. We come to consider historic Christian and Methodist teachings on the Holy Spirit, then, in the context of a contemporary culture that is, on the one hand, increasingly disinterested in religious organizations and institutions, and yet paradoxically fascinated with spirituality in a multiplicity of forms.

Sacred Presence in Historic Christian and Wesleyan Teachings

The third chapter considered the mystery of the Trinity, the mystery of one God known to us as Father, Son, and Holy Spirit. This chapter initiates our consideration of **the Holy Spirit**. There is more depth to consider here, although the church's teachings about the Holy Spirit have not always been explicit. The original version of the Nicene Creed (as adopted by the Council of Nicaea in A.D. 325) simply ends with the cryptic words "and [we believe] in the Holy Spirit." Debates about the divinity of the Holy Spirit in the 300s led the bishops at the first Council of Constantinople (A.D. 381) to expand this statement to say:

> and in the Holy Spirit, the Lord and Life-giver, who proceeds from the Father, who with the Father and the Son is worshiped and glorified, who spoke by the Prophets.

This clarified the belief that the Holy Spirit is equally and eternally God, along with the divine Persons of the Father and the Son. Eastern and Western churches later argued over this article of the creed, after the Western church altered it to say that the Spirit "proceeds from the Father *and the Son*." But this controversy was really

47

not so much over the nature of the Holy Spirit as it was about the nature of Christ, and the relationships between the Persons of the Trinity.

Subsequent discussions of the doctrine of the Trinity made an important point about the work of the Holy Spirit. When scriptures speak of the work of the Spirit (for example, in Romans 8:26), **we must not think that the Spirit speaks or works apart from the Father and the Son**. In fact, as Paul elaborates this idea in Romans 8, he makes the point that all the Persons of the Trinity are involved in leading us in prayer: The Son prays "Abba" to the Father, and the Spirit makes our prayer one with his. As Christians considered the meaning of this, they concluded that all of the works of the Trinity are performed by the whole Godhead in unity. Thus, although we may speak of the work of the Holy Spirit inspiring people or renewing the church, we must remember that this is a shorthand (and biblical) way of saying that God does these works, Father, Son, and Holy Spirit working together in unity.

A sensitive issue related to the understanding of the work of the Spirit has to do with our reverence for **the Spirit's work in the long history of the Christian church**. In their zeal for reformation, Protestants sometimes represented the Middle Ages as ages of debased superstition, and this led some Protestants to question or even deny the work of the Holy Spirit in the whole history of the church. This is a sensitive issue because it has the effect of making the older Christian traditions, especially Roman Catholic and Eastern Orthodox traditions, appear to be sub-Christian or cultic. Very often this was the result simply of ignorance of what had happened in this history. Who could know the story of St. Francis of Assisi, and deny the work of the Spirit in his life or in the Franciscan movement? Who could read Thomas à Kempis's *Imitation of Christ* and fail to sense the presence of the Spirit in his piety?

John Wesley responded on one occasion to the accusation that he was a "Papist" (Roman Catholic) in the following manner:

"Oh, but Mr. Hervey says *you* are *half* a Papist." What if he had *proved* it too? What if he had proved I was *whole* Papist? (though he might as easily have proved me a Mahometan). Is not a Papist a child of God? Is Thomas à Kempis, Mr. De Renty, Gregory Lopez gone to hell? Believe it who can. Yet still of such (though Papists) the same is my brother and sister and mother. (John Wesley, letter to John Newton, 9 April 1765; in the Telford edition of Wesley's *Letters*, 4:293)

Consistent with this point of view, Wesley elsewhere expressed his belief that the Spirit had inspired holy men and women through the history of the church, including the Middle Ages. We must be careful not to think in ways that limit the work of the Spirit, especially when we consider Christian traditions that are different from our own.

But don't take these comments of John Wesley to mean that he wasn't concerned with the lack of spiritual activity in the church. One of the reasons why Wesley was concerned about this was because of **the prominent role of the work of the Holy Spirit** that he perceived **in the Methodist movement**, which contrasted with deep suspicion of claims to inspiration by the Spirit in Wesley's Anglican Church. Wesley noted in his *Journal* on one occasion his conclusion:

That the grand reason why the miraculous gifts were so soon withdrawn [in the early church], was not only that faith and holiness were well nigh lost, but that dry, formal, orthodox men began even then to ridicule whatever gifts they had not themselves, and to decry them all as either madness or imposture. (Wesley's *Journal* for 15 August 1750; in the edition of Nehemiah Curnock 3:490)

Methodists spoke regularly of the work of the Spirit: in convicting sinners, in bringing sinners to faith in Christ, in giving the witness of the Spirit that our sins are forgiven, and in sanctifying believers.

With this belief in the work of the Spirit, John Wesley acted as **a kind of scientist of the religious life**. He interviewed people about their religious experiences, and took careful notes on his own and other people's experience. He and the Methodists after him developed a rich vocabulary for describing spiritual experiences. The titles of John Wesley's *Standard Sermons* give the terms they used to describe some of these experiences: "The Wilderness State,"

"Heaviness through Manifold Temptations," "Wandering Thoughts," and "The Witness of the Spirit." Methodist people often kept diaries, and in their classes and bands and societies often probed each other's experiences. **Personal testimony** became a hallmark of the Methodist movement. Methodist revivals in the 1800s regularly kept an account of how many persons were "awakened," "converted," and "sanctified" at the meeting. It is not surprising the Holiness and Pentecostal movements developed this emphasis on the work of the Spirit that was so much a part of early Methodism.

Throughout the history of the Christian church, then, teachings about the Holy Spirit have not been technically elaborated, but the long tradition of the Christian church has insisted on the abiding presence of the Holy Spirit. The Wesleyan movement made the work of the Holy Spirit a central focus in understanding the religious experience of men and women. But despite the interest in religious experience today, we seldom find occasions as Wesleyans or United Methodists to engage this prominent facet of our own tradition. The world, and even our churches, often seem disconnected from the work of the Spirit.

The Loss of the Sacred

In fact, interpreters of contemporary society often refer to **"the loss of the sacred"** in our times. "Is nothing sacred anymore?" It appears that for many of our contemporaries, life has simply lost the sense of wonder and mystery and sacredness that it has held for men and women in the past. Here we must try to understand this pervasive sense of the "loss of the sacred" in contemporary life.

It is tempting to say that the "loss of the sacred" is the result of **the conflict of science and religion**. In fact, many historical interpreters through the 1930s believed that religion and science are enemies by nature, and that a scientific outlook on the world cannot be consistent with a religious outlook. This point of view was challenged from the 1930s by Columbia University historian Robert Merton and others who pointed out that Protestantism was the seedbed from which modern observational science grew. John

Wesley, we might note in this regard, was fascinated with scientific developments, and carried out his own electrical experiments, much like his contemporary Benjamin Franklin. He did not seem to sense any contradiction between these scientific pursuits and his religious convictions. The opposition or "warfare" of science and religion really developed in the 1800s.

Perhaps, then, we should say that it is not the conflict of science and religion that led to a loss of a sense of the sacred, but it was a very particular idea that grew along with the scientific worldview. That idea was **the pervasive notion that purely mechanical or material observations could explain everything about the universe.** Even if science had not yet explained everything, the belief went, the steady progress of science had shown countless earlier superstitions to be false, and would eventually offer a total explanation of every facet of the universe. This belief is often described as belief in a "closed universe," that is, the material universe is a "closed" system that does not require any external intervention from a God, gods, or other spiritual beings, to account for it. Ludwig Feuerbach reduced it to a simple slogan: *Man ist was er isst,* "one is what one eats." Material reality, on this view, is simply all there is.

Before dismissing the notion of a closed universe, we should pause to consider **how pervasive this idea has become.** It is not just that a particular ideology is taught in schools and universities; what is hugely pervasive in the modern world is simply the absence of the traditional understanding that the universe is a vast and mysterious place, shot through with divinity in every part. We have to admit that we do not regularly expect (or even pray for) divine intervention in the mundane events of everyday life, as our great grandparents and earlier forebears did. Modern literature and media offer (purportedly) objective accounts of events, with no reference at all to divine providence.

So when we speak of the "loss of the sacred," we are not speaking of the province of intellectuals and scientists. We mean that **modern life,** including our own lives (we confess), **is largely lived without a consciousness of the presence of God's Holy Spirit.** And we mean (and this is perhaps most telling) that our churches often betray very little sense of immediate divine presence. Chapter

9 will consider in more depth the effect that this has had on Christian worship. Here we are concerned with the broader issue of the "loss of the sacred," and the challenge that this poses to our churches and to the Wesleyan heritage today.

The Holy Spirit and the Spirit of the Age

The reader must note a certain tension between what has been said here about the "loss of the sacred" in the previous section and the claim in the introduction to this unit that modern women and men regularly have experiences that they themselves identify as "religious" in some way. We can think of no easy way to resolve this. **Both claims seem to be true:** Modern people do not regularly think in terms of divine intervention, and yet modern people regularly have experiences that challenge them with the tantalizing possibility of spiritual realities. In this section, we come to consider at least three reasons why belief in the present power of the Holy Spirit may make sense, even to contemporary people who have been deeply affected by the loss of a sense of the sacred.

First, we should say that **scientific thought itself in the past century betrayed some hints of a larger reality**. Early in the twentieth century, an "uncertainty principle" or "indeterminacy principle" was proposed, according to which the precise position and velocity of a subatomic particle can never be determined at the same time with complete accuracy. To some, this seemed to question on scientific grounds the notion of a closed universe. It led to Alfred North Whitehead's creative construction of a "process" philosophy, and this in turn led to a whole school of Christian speculation sometimes called "process theology," in which Methodists (such as Schubert M. Ogden and John B. Cobb Jr.) were prominent. At some points, then, scientific investigation itself called into question the materialism it had fostered.

Second, despite the stunning developments in science and technology through the twentieth century, **scientific and technological developments raised critical moral issues that scientific learning by itself seemed quite unprepared to address**. Men and women in the nineteenth century could have believed that scientific progress was inevitably linked to moral progress. But the twentieth century witnessed a series of horrors delivered by modern technology, such as massively efficient weapons systems and environmental destruction brought about by industrial processes. Medical technologies and advances that extended our life spans gave the world the luxury of surviving chronic diseases that almost always led to death for our ancestors, and these very developments have choked systems that deliver crucial medical aid. Science by itself seems morally cursed, and newer scientific developments such as genetic manipulation pose even more difficult moral issues.

Third, the questioning of dominant cultures in the twentieth century meant, above all, a questioning of the dominant scientific outlook that characterized the Western world. The second half of the twentieth century saw the flourishing in the Western world of **alternative philosophies**: "New Age" religion, alternative forms of medical treatment, and even alternative technologies. The multicultural societies that emerged in this same period have brought into the modern world the presence of **older religious and spiritual traditions**, including such Eastern religious traditions as Buddhism and Hinduism, and revitalized older European traditions, such as those of Celtic peoples (both Christian and pagan). The presence of the Internet has only encouraged the proliferation of these varied philosophical and religious perspectives. The world in which we live now, as contrasted with the world of 1950, is a world alive with spiritual visions; however they may exist in an uneasy tension with scientific materialism.

Conclusion: Living in the Spirit's Presence Today

The supreme irony of our own time might be that although the world outside of our churches seems to have developed an intense fascination with the spiritual, it is **finding very little in our traditional churches to feed its spiritual interest**. This irony is particularly damning for churches in the Wesleyan tradition, given what we have said above about the prominence of religious experience and belief in the present power of the Holy Spirit in our tradition. Christianity cannot become a "designer religion" determined by contemporary fads and interests, but woe to us if we fail to discern the spiritual aspirations of our own times, and if we fail to offer the spiritual riches of our heritage in this age. It might be that we ourselves are in danger of failing to discern the mystery of the Spirit's presence.

Wesleyan Christians need to recover our own tradition's rich vocabulary for describing spiritual experience. That will be the subject of chapter 7 and other parts of this study series. We need to recover a sense of divine presence in worship (the subject of chapter 9). We also need to recover **the art of "Christian conversation,"** the ability to speak to each other about spiritual experiences. These do not need to be particularly vivid or earth-shattering experiences, but Christians will find it difficult to speak to the world outside of the church about our religious experiences if we have not shared within our own communities of faith how we have experienced the Spirit's reality in our own lives.

If there is such a great hunger for spirituality in our contemporary multicultural world, Wesleyan Christians need to offer the hidden gifts of our own heritage. The historic Wesleyan emphasis on the present reality of the Holy Spirit, our stress on the need for personal religious experience, even our historic and "technical" language for describing the work of the Spirit, are great gifts to be shared in our contemporary world. Through our sisters and brothers in Holiness and Pentecostal churches, those gifts have been shared even more broadly in the world. Our understanding of the Spirit's work is gifts bestowed upon us by God, and "we have received not the spirit of the world, but the Spirit that is from God, so that we may understand the gifts bestowed on us by God" (1 Corinthians 2:12).

QUESTIONS FOR DISCUSSION

1. Why might a scientific view of the world lead to a loss of the sense of the sacred?
2. In your experience, do people in your world think of the world in entirely materialistic terms, or do they recognize spiritual realities?

3. What opportunities have you had to hear other persons—Christian or non-Christian—describe their religious experiences?
4. Would a visitor to your congregation, or to your Sunday school class, have a sense of God's presence there?

CHAPTER 6

Does Humanity
Need God?

Just as I am, without one plea... (Charlotte Elliott)

Introduction

It does not take rocket science to observe the human situation and confirm that there is something desperately and fundamentally wrong with humanity. All of the tremendous and phenomenal advances of knowledge and science have not deterred the violence and evil that human beings perpetrate on one another and their world. In the 1800s people may have believed that things were getting better and better, but the events of the twentieth century seem to have negated those romantic hopes. Just watch the evening news and little doubt can remain about humanity's predicament. How do we address and respond to these complex crises of violence, disaster, corruption, and personal chaos from a Wesleyan perspective, and with a redemptive influence? Historically, Methodists and the Wesleyan tradition have emphasized the optimism of divine grace. The Bible holds out the hope of God's transforming presence and power for personal and societal change.

Self-help seminars, Twelve Step programs, and "I'm OK, You're OK" philosophies, though they may be helpful to overcome low self-esteem, addictions, and compulsive behaviors, often fail to take into account the need for a radical transformation of our essential humanity. (As we shall see, some of these in fact reflect the earlier influence of Methodist societies and means of behavior modification.) While these "helps" may improve the quality of our lives, they do not address or deal with the issues of sin, guilt, and reconciliation to God: What must I do to be saved? There exists an incomparable difference in believing in a generic "higher power" and a personal relationship with Jesus Christ that reorders all of life.

Fallen Humanity

The Bible describes humanity as fallen, separated from God, and having a sinful nature—a propensity to sin. The Bible suggests that human morality and in fact what it means to be human are grounded in an understanding of God rather than a purely psychological foundation. Optimistic anthropology focuses on the human ability to change and improve: On this view, human beings are believed to have within themselves the potential for improvement. Methodism's historic doctrinal position is that human beings cannot save themselves and stand in need of God's grace. God's assistance and intervention is required. Wesleyans do not devalue or denigrate the sanctity or worth of human beings. Human beings are of infinite value to God. "For God so loved the world that he gave his only Son, so that everyone who believes in him may not perish but may have eternal life. Indeed, God did not send the Son into the world to condemn the world, but in order that the world might be saved through him" (John 3:16-17).

Historical Christian teachings about human nature and salvation attempt to describe this sinful or fallen condition of humankind, and God's intention for the healing of the condition. These issues were at the forefront of the Protestant Reformation, and Methodists and the broader Wesleyan evangelical tradition inherited these views from the Reformation. John Wesley made some distinctive contributions to the foundational teachings about human nature and salvation. Wesley rejected the optimistic anthropology of the Enlightenment that suggested that human beings have an innate (inborn) ability to improve or save themselves. One of his most profound contributions to the dilemma of the human predicament was his understanding of optimistic grace. In the Wesleyan understanding, grace defines and clarifies what it means to be human.

What Does It Mean to Be Human?

A Christian view of humanity always sees humanity in relation to God. Human beings, according to John Wesley, are the only creatures "capable of God." "So God created humankind in his image, in the image of God he created them; male and female he created them" (Genesis 1:27). Theologians throughout the centuries have attempted to locate this divine image as "some thing" within human beings. Created in the image and likeness of God is not meant to explain what God is like, but rather how human beings are related to God. The divine image (*imago Dei*) cannot be defined simply as something within humanity such as reason/intellect or physical attributes. It is not a natural capacity. It is better understood as a relationship in which humans stand.

Humans, created in the image of God, were created in original righteousness. They were endowed with perfect righteousness and holiness. Wesley calls this "original perfection." In his sermon on "The Image of God," Wesley defines this perfection in terms of perfect understanding, perfect freedom, and a perfect will. Human beings were free from error, knowing right from wrong. The motivating affection of their lives was love, and they were endowed with the freedom to choose and determine their lives.

As a consequence of the Fall, the natural image of God was defaced and radically damaged, but not totally destroyed. However, the moral image defined as true righteousness and holiness with the constitutive freedom of choosing good or evil was lost. This corruption resulted in alienation from God, a habitual inclination toward evil, and the loss of the freedom to obey God. The knowledge of God was lost. Human will was ruled by pride and self-centered affections, rather than by love.

The Doctrine of Original Sin

Wesley held a twofold view of sin, distinguishing between sin as a nature and sin as a personal act. Sin as a propensity or nature, is referred to as *original sin*. The discussion of sin as a personal act will be pursued later.

Original sin is a universal characteristic of humanity. Human beings became slaves to sin. The implication of the doctrine of original sin is that the nature of every person is corrupt. The primary effect of original sin is the loss of freedom; it renders human beings free only to sin. The Methodists' seventh Article of Religion states that original sin marks a fall from original righteousness. Humanity's freedom for righteousness and true holiness is impaired by original sin. In his sermon on "Original Sin" Wesley wrote that all have sinned, and that there exists a common participation in Adam's original sin. In some manner we all died in Adam, and we are all subject to moral and spiritual defect.

When does a human being actually become depraved? Human beings do not become depraved upon the first act of sin, but commit sin because they have a sinful tendency. Human beings are born into this world corrupted. Charles Wesley's hymn "Love Divine, All Loves Excelling" describes this tendency as humanity's "bent to sinning." Genesis 3 details the disobedience and consequent fall of humanity, and then in Genesis 6:5 the universality of sin is described: "The LORD saw that the wickedness of humankind was great in the earth, and that every inclination of the thoughts of their hearts was only evil continually." Sin impairs the human freedom to make moral choices.

Universal sinfulness is the inheritance of every child of Adam and Eve. Fallen humanity suffers complete corruption—every part of life is touched and tainted by sin. This infection of sin touches every human being and every human being lives in a world infected by sin. No part of human existence escapes the corruption of the sinful nature. The teaching of the Scripture is that all persons are born into this world separated from the life of God. Psalm 51:5 reinforces this thought: "Indeed, I was born guilty, a sinner when my mother conceived me." How this sinful nature is transmitted from our first human parents remains a mystery to us, but it is apparent that something occurred that has affected the whole human race.

However, John Wesley believed that no one would be eternally condemned because of Adam and Eve's disobedience. The sinful nature, unaided by grace, results in actual sin, that is, sin for which we are actually responsible and for which we are liable to God's judgment. The condition of the natural human being is spiritual death, there is no admission or recognition of sinfulness. Human beings become culpable when they yield to the sinful nature, commit actual sin, and then reject the remedy. Wesley believed that every human being falls into actual sin, and therefore there exists a universal need for grace. The denial of original sin is to refute the foundational truth of Christianity, the need for salvation.

Actual Sin

Although contemporary society might prefer to deny the objective reality of sin, Christians have historically believed that our inclination or "bent to sinning" leads to actual sins. We commit sin (actual sin) because we are sinners (by nature). Or, put in a slightly different way, the result of our sinful condition is the committing of actual sin. Wesley attempted to define sin in relational terms that have caused some confusion and controversy. Distinguishing between original sin and actual sin, Wesley defined the latter (he also called it "sin, properly understood") as "a voluntary transgression of a known law of God." Actual sin involves moral choice and responsibility and knowledge of the divine law. Actual sin can also be understood as a violation of the law of love, that is, the Great Commandment to love God with all that we are, and the related commandment to love our neighbors as ourselves.

Applying this definition of sin to a perfect standard of conduct to which all humanity falls short proves very difficult. The residual effects of the Fall are such that no person is capable of perfect thinking, emotion, or performance. The definition is workable and helpful when sin is understood as a matter of intention and relationship. The primary concern of Wesley is the motive of the heart (the will). However, this does not diminish or lessen the necessity for correct conduct or behavior. Sinful actions and attitudes are the result of a self-centered, selfish pride, a violation of love.

It is not enough to deal with sin in a legal and juridical manner. Sin is more than just a state of rebellion and separation from God.

Albert Outler reminds us that Wesley viewed sin as a malignant disease. Sin is a sickness of the soul shown in an absence of love, and this sickness needs to be healed, "since all have sinned and fall short of the glory of God" (Romans 3:23; also see Romans 6:15-23 and 1 John 1:9–2:4). Wesley declares "that Adam, before his fall, had such freedom of will, that he might choose either good or evil; but that, since the fall, no child of man has a natural power to choose anything that is truly good."

Wesley did not exalt humanity's natural abilities. Free moral choice has been lost. Fallen humanity is free only to sin and has no power or will to choose good or to perform it. Human beings cannot perform their way into God's favor, they cannot come to God on their own. There is the need of divine grace to start the work of salvation in human beings. Therefore, God has not left humanity to its own resourcefulness to save itself. "Therefore, just as sin came into the world through one man, and death came through sin, and so death spread to all, because all sinned. . . . Therefore just as one man's trespass led to condemnation for all, so one man's act of righteousness leads to justification and life for all" (Romans 5:12, 18). This act of righteousness makes the free gift of grace available to all.

The Doctrine of Grace

UNIVERSAL GRACE

It was Wesley's doctrine of universal grace that forced him into the area of religious controversy over the issues of predestination, election, and human responsibility. Wesley rejected any notion of a "limited atonement," a corollary of predestination that maintained that only a "limited number" of persons, determined by God before the ages, could be saved. Wesley's belief that *all* might be saved resulted in his theological insistence on free and universal grace. Wesley substantiates this view in his sermon on "Free Grace." He wrote:

> How freely does God love the world! While we were yet sinners, "Christ died for the ungodly." While we were "dead in sin," God

"spared not his own Son, but delivered him up for us all." And how freely with him does he "give us all things"! Verily, free grace is all in all! The grace or love of God, whence cometh our salvation, is free in all, and free for all. ("Free Grace," based on Romans 8:32)

Wesley insisted that grace was universally available—and that salvation is possible for everyone. It is not limited to a specific number of human beings elected or chosen by God for salvation. In today's multicultural society it is imperative for Wesleyans to make clear our belief that God offers salvation to everyone. No one is excluded from the love of God by an eternal decree: "He is patient with you, not wanting anyone to perish, but all to come to repentance" (2 Peter 3:9).

Salvation for Wesley involved the initiating grace of God and the appropriation of that grace, through faith, on the part of the believer. Wesley's doctrine of salvation is by grace alone while at the same time giving a place for the response of the human will. This cooperant grace holds in tension the divine sovereignty of God and human responsibility, and maintains the integrity of both. Wesley's most significant contribution to reformation theology was his synthesis of grace, faith, free will, and the sovereignty of God.

TWOFOLD GRACE

Wesley's doctrine of twofold grace brings together God's sovereignty and humanity's free will. As articulated by Wesley, grace must always be understood as God's grace. God is always the modifier of the concept and doctrine of grace. Grace is God seeking us, not our finding God. God through the gifts of grace and faith makes possible our response to God's overture of salvation. Grace is God's gracious redemptive action toward us in Christ. Grace is the saving work (redemption) of a holy, living God through the life and death of Jesus Christ by the power of the Holy Spirit. Wesley's concept of grace moves beyond grace as a state (or thing) to grace as a dynamic relationship.

Wesley postulates grace as first, divine favor (approval) and acceptance, and second, as the empowerment by the Holy Spirit. Biblical grace is real and transforming. It is not cheap grace; it is costly, but free. It does not allow just for forgiveness and leave the sinners in their desperate condition of sinfulness. Grace emphasizes God's possibilities rather than humanity's incapacity or limitation. The change, in Wesley's view, was real as well as relative. Grace makes possible a change in the state of our relationship with God, and makes possible an authentic change in our person. We are inwardly renewed and outwardly changed by the power of God. It is not illusory grace but real, present grace, and it has real effects. Grace, God's love in action, is mediated to us through the Holy Spirit. The Holy Spirit is God's active agent of grace.

THE THREEFOLD MOVEMENT OF RESTORING GRACE

Wesley's doctrine of grace can be unpacked with greater specificity and degrees, but the major components of Wesley's doctrine are found in three movements: *prevenient grace; justifying grace; and sanctifying grace.* Each of these three movements will be considered in the next chapter as we show the distinctive character of Wesleyan spirituality. But even here we need to say more about prevenient grace.

PREVENIENT GRACE

Wesley's concept of grace is a critical reconstruction of the Christian understanding of grace. According to Wesley, grace is prevenient and cooperative. Prevenient grace (or "preventing grace" in Wesley's eighteenth-century usage) is God's grace that comes to us before we believe in Christ. The Wesleyan tradition has consistently maintained that prevenient grace is God's grace given to every human being. Thus, whenever any human being does good (Christian or not), we rejoice in the presence of divine grace.

Wesley's doctrine of prevenient grace is not an abstract concept. Rather, it is an expression of his faith in the universal plan of redemption of God in Christ. The doctrine of election or predestination was displaced by Wesley's concept of prevenient grace. Wesley disagreed with the Calvinists' understanding of predestination, election, and the irresistibility of grace. He did believe in the sovereignty of God, and he also recognized humanity's inherent incapacity to save itself, but his concept of grace resulted in some divergent anthropological conclusions about original sin and total depravity, and free will (as already noted). Wesley held that grace does not act irresistibly, but in fact, beyond prevenient grace it can be not only resisted, but also finally refused. Prevenient grace is a divine-human encounter involving the offer of grace on God's part and the genuine possibility of accepting or rejecting this grace on the part of human beings.

Wesley understood that even prevenient grace is a benefit of the atoning work of Christ. Prevenient grace, like all grace, is a free gift. With God's initiating grace we are free to respond to God's invitation of salvation in Christ. Prevenient grace awakens human beings to their sinful condition and their need of salvation. Though Wesley held to the view of total depravity, he believed that there was no person without divine prevenient grace. Wesley maintained in a letter to Mr. John Mason, November 21, 1776, that although humans cannot make any self-move toward God, "no man living is without some preventing grace, and every degree of grace is a degree of life."

In the Wesleyan understanding, no one is saved by prevenient grace itself; Wesley used this term to describe grace coming before our believing in Christ. Humans must appropriate (make their own) the atoning work of Christ through faith. Faith is not a human possibility apart from God. Salvation is the entire work of God. Human beings are incapable of altering their condition. Both grace and faith are gifts of God through the active presence of the Holy Spirit.

It is the working of the Holy Spirit that convicts of sin and convinces the sinner of their sinfulness. In Wesleyan theology there is a high priority given to the present work of the Holy Spirit, as noted in chapter 5. Wesley makes the Holy Spirit and the grace of God almost interchangeable in practice. The Holy Spirit is the source and the initiator of the ability to respond to God's offer of forgiveness. The Holy Spirit is working in the lives of all people, whether Christian or not. Through the Holy Spirit, one is made acutely aware of one's sins, made conscious of the compassion of a holy

God, and one is resolutely faced with the decision to choose light or darkness, either life or death. In plain words, grace works to call us to repent and trust Christ.

This convincing grace through faith and trust in the atoning work of Christ becomes converting grace through the empowering, renewing presence of the Holy Spirit. For Wesley salvation does not happen outside of Christ. The gospel message was salvation by grace through faith alone. By faith in Christ our justification and new birth are made possible.

This understanding of prevenient grace has radical implications for Christians living in a multicultural world. Good News! Christ is already at work in our multicultural world. We do not need to think of ourselves as initiating the work of evangelism, or drawing persons to faith in Christ. We can trust that Christ is already at work in them. It is up to us to be faithful to the work that Christ has already begun through the Holy Spirit in them—and in us!

QUESTIONS FOR DISCUSSION

1. Do you believe that there is something fundamentally wrong with humanity? Are human beings capable of saving themselves? Is original sin a helpful explanation of fallenness?
2. How would you explain the *image of God* in humanity?
3. Do you agree with Wesley's twofold view of sin? What is the difference between sin as a nature and sin as an action. How is sin relational?
4. How was Wesley's view of grace radically different from the Reformers?
5. What is the twofold nature of grace?
6. Why is Wesley's doctrine of prevenient grace central to his theology?

CHAPTER 7

More than a Casual Relationship: Saving Grace

For by grace you have been saved through faith, and this is not your own doing; it is the gift of God. (Ephesians 2:8)

Introduction

We need to be clear about the gifts we have to offer to a multicultural world. Not everything in the European or American past is good, not everything in the Christian past is particularly good, and there is a good deal in the past history of Methodism that can be left to history. But there are also great treasures—we tend to call these our "heritage," that is, the things from the past that we value highly. **One of the treasures we have as Wesleyan Christians is a distinctive spirituality that focuses on our understanding of "the way of salvation."** This is one of the great treasures of our inheritance that we should share with our contemporary world, and this spirituality is the subject of this chapter.

The previous chapter makes clear the human need for divine grace or assistance. This historic Christian claim, as we have seen, often stands in an uneasy tension with claims that we are saved by doing what is right or by being good. Christians have historically claimed that by ourselves, unaided by grace, we cannot in fact do what is right and we cannot be good.

But how is it that we live out this belief in the saving grace of God? Here is where we encounter the treasures of the Wesleyan spiritual tradition. John and Charles Wesley developed an elaborate understanding of the working of divine grace, which they sometimes called "the way of salvation." They taught this distinct pattern of the Christian life through their hymns, their sermons, and through reflection on their own testimony (such as John Wesley's published *Journal*).

Sometimes John Wesley summarized the distinctive teachings of the Methodist movement with reference to Methodist teachings about "repentance, faith and holiness." Although the use of this particular vocabulary is not an essential of Christian faith, the rich elaboration of the "way of salvation" was a kind of Wesleyan and Methodist essential, something that united the Wesleyan movement and became one of Methodism's gifts to the whole Christian community. For the Wesleyan tradition, saving grace is "more than a casual relationship": It is a relationship in which we are called to ever richer growth into the divine image.

Historic Teachings on Salvation by Grace

Prior to the Protestant Reformation, there was a strong belief in the need for good works and faith in the Christian life. Protestants often misrepresented Catholics as teaching "works righteousness," but ecumenical discussions have shown that this was indeed a misrepresentation. It would be more accurate to say that many Catholic teachers in Luther's time believed that although we are saved by faith, we will not receive the gift of faith until we do everything within our own power. In the spirituality popular in Luther's time, this meant that human beings had to engage in works of charity (feeding the hungry, helping the poor) and works of piety (making a full and sincere confession of sin, attending mass, reciting such customary prayers as the "Lord's Prayer" and the "Hail Mary"). This spirituality laid a tremendous emphasis on the need for human works as being necessary prior to receiving the gifts of divine grace.

Luther reacted against this popular spirituality. If it wasn't explicitly works righteousness, he maintained, it *amounted* practically to works righteousness in its emphasis on the importance of human works in salvation. Luther insisted that salvation must be entirely the work of divine grace: The expression *sola gratia* ("by grace alone") summarizes this foundational Protestant principle. Luther emphasized **justification** as the divine act by which humans are forgiven through faith in Christ. Our salvation, then, is also *sola fide*, "by faith alone," but Luther insisted that faith itself is a gift of grace, not a human act (see chapter 6). It might be important to notice that one of the accomplishments of twentieth-century ecumenical discussions was that Catholics and Lutherans came to understand each other better on this point. Catholics made more explicit their belief that salvation is always the gift of grace; Lutherans made it clear that what Luther had attacked was not Catholicism as a whole, but a very particular form of late-medieval Catholicism. The "Joint Declaration on Justification" signed by Lutheran and Catholic leaders on October 31, 1999, made public the results of these long discussions.

Whereas Luther placed primary emphasis on justification or forgiveness, the **Reformed tradition**, which began with the reforming work of Ulrich Zwingli and John Calvin and includes modern Congregationalist and Presbyterian churches, developed a broader concern for the ways in which grace affects the whole life of a Christian. Reformed teachers developed a particular pattern for describing the work of grace based on Romans 8:30. According to this pattern, which Reformed teachers described as the **"order of salvation,"** Christians pass through the following stages or moments in the Christian life:

Effectual calling or **vocation**, when a person is called to follow Christ; this is usually accompanied by repentance and the recognition that one cannot save oneself;

Justification, when one's sins are forgiven through faith in Christ, usually accompanied in Reformed teaching by a divinely given "assurance" of "adoption," the spiritual knowledge that one has been forgiven and is included among the elect;

Sanctification, when the believer is made progressively more holy by "mortification" (death to sin) and "vivification" (life following the example of Christ); and

Glorification, when, after the believer's death, the Christian enters into the blissful fellowship of Christ and the saints.

Reformed Christians, including English Puritans, used this pattern to describe their own experiences in spiritual diaries, biographies, and autobiographies. John Bunyan used it to describe his own life in *Grace Abounding to the Chief of Sinners* and then to describe the life of a Christian "pilgrim" in his vividly imaginative allegory of *The Pilgrim's Progress from This World to the Next* (1678). Presbyterian communion celebrations, extended over several days, enacted this pattern by preaching through each phase of this "order of salvation." These celebrations lay in the background of later American camp meetings.

The Wesleyan Contribution

John Wesley's careful observation of his own spiritual life and the spiritual experiences of others (see chapter 5) led him to adopt a somewhat altered version of this understanding of the **"way of salvation"** (the term he preferred). As we have seen in chapter 6, Wesley rejected the belief in predestination or election that had been a crucial element in the Reformed understanding of the Christian life. Wesley saw grace as part of the divine-human relationship, since it was based on God's prior love for all of humankind. His pattern for understanding the spiritual life was described in a number of different ways, but three consistent elements of the Wesleyan pattern are as follows:

Prevenient grace, which means God's grace "coming before" (Latin, *preveniens*) our believing in Christ and preparing us for justification by giving us power to believe and by leading us to repentance and a desire to please God;

Justifying grace, which means the grace by which God forgives our sins through faith in Christ, and which (Wesley believed) is normally accompanied by a divinely given "assurance of pardon"; and

Sanctifying grace, God's grace through which the believer is made progressively more holy following Christ's example until the moment when (again by grace) she or he loves God completely (Christian perfection).

This pattern is repeated throughout Wesleyan and Methodist spiritual literature. For example, the current (1989) *United Methodist Hymnal* has a long section describing the Christian life using the headings "Prevenient Grace" (hymns 337-359), "Justifying Grace" (hymns 361-381), and "Sanctifying and Perfecting Grace" (hymns 382-536).

This pattern of spiritual life is so crucial for the Wesleyan tradition that we should elaborate on each of its parts. Each of these phases of the spiritual life was accompanied by religious experiences that were signs of the working of grace. The period of **prevenient grace** has been described in the previous unit. Here let us note that Wesleyans understood that this phase of spiritual life was accompanied by horror at the thought of sin and judgment, sometimes expressed by persons shouting aloud or trembling with fear, and by the beginning of a desire to please God. Methodists often testified to a terrifying experience of "awakening," when they realized the danger of their souls before God. Methodist preachers stressed the importance of God's law at this point to convince persons of their shortcomings and their need for grace. Consistent with their belief in the universal availability of grace (chapter 6), Methodists held that prevenient grace had been made available to every person: Christ is "the true light, which enlightens everyone" (John 1:9*a*). So Charles Wesley sang,

> Come, sinners, to the gospel feast;
>   let every soul be Jesus' guest.
> Ye need not one be left behind,
>   for God hath bid all humankind.
> (*United Methodist Hymnal*, no. 339)

Justifying grace denoted God's grace that forgives our sins based on faith in Christ's work. "Faith," John Wesley explained, is not simply intellectual assent, it involves heartfelt trust in Christ. Although he later allowed exceptional cases, John Wesley believed that faith and justification were normally accompanied by the "blessed assurance" of sins forgiven, and early Methodist literature is filled with testimonies to the "witness of the Spirit" that one's sins were forgiven. Some of Charles Wesley's most dramatic verse expresses this idea, including this poem, which Charles is believed to have written shortly after his own experience of conversion in May 1738:

> O how shall I the goodness tell,
> Father, which thou to me hast showed?
> That I, a child of wrath and hell,
> I should be called a child of God!
> Should know, should feel my sins forgiven,
> blest with this antepast [foretaste] of heaven!
> (*United Methodist Hymnal*, no. 342)

Sanctifying grace denoted God's grace leading the believer to greater and greater holiness. In this process, a believer's desires are purified until the believer finally loves what God loves, desires what God desires. The Great Commandment is the fulfillment of entire sanctification, and it too (like justification) is a work of divine grace. In Wesleyan teaching, the process of sanctification was marked by the trials and temptations of the believer, moments of grace to strengthen the believer, particular spiritual problems faced by believers, and also the joy of fellowship or communion with the Savior. As we shall see in chapter 8, it leads believers to entire sanctification or Christian perfection, complete or perfect love for God. Again, Charles Wesley's hymns often described the process of sanctification and the "second rest" of entire sanctification:

> Breathe, O breathe thy loving Spirit into every troubled breast!
> Let us all in thee inherit; let us find that second rest.
> Take away our bent to sinning; Alpha and Omega be;
> End of faith, as its beginning, set our hearts at liberty.
> (*United Methodist Hymnal*, no. 384)

71

Understanding the spiritual journey in this fashion was a hallmark of Methodist piety. Methodist revivals and camp meetings were often organized in such a way as to lead persons through this map of the spiritual life. The pattern persisted, at least in some Methodist circles, well into the twentieth century. For example, progressive United Methodist Bishop James K. Mathews's autobiography, *A Global Odyssey* (Abingdon Press, 2000), recounts his own experiences of conversion and assurance (which he calls "the witness of the Spirit" in traditional Wesleyan language), and his quest for personal and social holiness.

Grace in an Age of Casual Relationships

Although this pattern persisted into the twentieth century, Methodists have not been consistently formed in this pattern of spirituality in recent decades. Some of the terms may be familiar, but even when Methodists have heard about "justification" or "sanctification," they are seldom placed in the framework of this historic understanding of the "way of salvation." It would be tempting to ascribe this entirely to the increasing secularization of society (chapter 5), but even within the evangelical Christian community, this rich understanding of the way of salvation has been flattened into a one-step process of becoming a Christian through a conversion experience. Both the prior sense of sin and the need for grace (which Methodists understood as the work of prevenient grace) and the subsequent process of sanctification tend to be neglected in contemporary evangelical spirituality. Divine grace, even for evangelical Christians, can become a casual relationship, a one-night-stand with Jesus.

Early in the twentieth century **the older emphasis on sin (and the dangers of hell) began to disappear** quietly from evangelical revivals. The "mourner's bench" so prominent in earlier camp meetings remained in many places, but its meaning was largely forgotten. Evangelicals were probably influenced (perhaps more than they realized) by a popular liberalism that accentuated the positive and downplayed such negative topics as sin and divine judgment. Revivals began to emphasize the urgency of conversion, but without the expectation that a person might spend a considerable amount of time in spiritual struggle prior to conversion. Denying what had been a consistent part of Christian nurture impoverished evangelical spirituality.

Similarly, **twentieth-century revivals often downplayed the importance of sanctification** or growth in holiness following conversion. It has been especially difficult for parachurch evangelistic organizations to link new believers with Christian communities where they can be formed in Christian faith and discipline. Without the expectation of commitment to a Christian community, mass evangelism could become a kind of ritualized absolution: walk down to the front, say the sinner's prayer with a counselor, go home on the bus, mark it up on the records as a "conversion," and presto! your Christian life is done. Even within holiness churches, entire sanctification could be emphasized apart from the life-changing process of growth in holiness (see chapter 8). In this way, too, the richness of the "way of salvation" could be diminished. Too often, entire sanctification was viewed as a "completed work" rather than the culmination of a life of continual growth.

But give evangelicals credit, at least, for maintaining the centrality of conversion. In many instances, **conversion simply disappeared** from the Methodist vocabulary. Many Methodists in the twentieth century came to regard conversion as the unique province of Baptists or other evangelicals. Moreover, by the 1960s Methodists had formally taken up the language of **confirmation** used historically by Catholics, Anglicans, Lutherans, Presbyterians, and other historic Christian traditions. The practice of confirmation allowed Christian initiation, in some places, to become a matter of classroom learning followed by a ritual of reception into the church. Where this was done at a prescribed age, it could be the result of peer pressure or parental pressure rather than a genuine change of heart and a personal decision to profess the faith into which one had been baptized. Although there was no formal reason why confirmation should have been disconnected from the expectation of conversion, the manner in which confirmation was practiced often did lead to such a disconnection.

Conclusion: Talking About the Way of Salvation Today

Given the richness of our heritage and the manner in which it has become impoverished in the last century, **we must suggest two things** for contemporary Wesleyan Christians. First, we need to relearn and reappropriate this inheritance. But second, we also need to be sensitive to new ways in which men and women may describe their experience of the divine and their spiritual journeys today.

We do need to relearn the Wesleyan inheritance about the "way of salvation." Although the language of John Wesley's *Standard Sermons* is sometimes difficult for our contemporaries, they are the classic source of understanding this spiritual tradition. (Kenneth Kinghorn's reformulated *Standard Sermons,* written in contemporary language, may be helpful.) The sermon entitled "The Scripture Way of Salvation" offers an overview of John Wesley's understanding of the spiritual journey, and might make a good starting point for discussion. Second to John Wesley's sermons are the hymns of Charles Wesley. Most Methodist hymnals have a long section describing the Christian life, including numerous hymns from Charles Wesley and others. It will be helpful to work through this section of the hymnal (see the notes above on the *United Methodist Hymnal*), asking how each of the hymns reflects an aspect of the spiritual journey under its appropriate heading.

We also need to learn the Wesleyan inheritance about the way of salvation **by asking how our own lives reflect this pattern**. It is not of course necessary to utilize the particular terms that John Wesley and Methodists used, but we can ask how this traditional description of the spiritual journey may describe our experiences as Christians. Many Christians, including non-Wesleyans, who are exposed to the Wesleyan teaching about the way of salvation can immediately understand aspects of their own spiritual lives in it. "Aha!" they will say, "God was leading me to conversion using such-and-such a person" (technical term: prevenient grace). We can use this pattern as a kind of spiritual mirror to examine our own lives. Sometimes it will reveal important, missing aspects of our own spiritual experience.

But the second thing we must advocate is **sensitivity to the different ways in which people may experience God** and the varied ways in which they may describe these experiences. John Wesley acted, as we have seen, as a kind of scientist of the Christian life. He was genuinely interested to hear people's stories. He sometimes even changed his own understanding of the way of salvation based on what people told him about their experiences. We should do the same today. We should approach other Christians and other people in general with a genuine curiosity about their religious walk, their own experiences, and even the ways in which they are able to express their experiences.

To take one example, because of the way in which sin and repentance have been understated in modern Christianity, **many Christians today will testify that they have been more aware of their own sin and unworthiness *after* their conversions** than before it. This stands in contrast to the older patterns (both Reformed and Wesleyan) where consciousness of sin almost always preceded conversion. But this is quite understandable in our own context: Many of our contemporaries grow up in a world that looks more like "Mr. Rogers' Neighborhood" than John Wesley's England, and for persons who have grown up in this way, awareness of sin may well follow personal commitment to Christ.

In a multicultural society, it will be even more important to be sensitive to people's varied experiences. Not only the vocabulary that the Wesleys used to describe the way of salvation, but the manner in which people experienced this was grounded in a particular culture in a particular period. Much of the language in which the Wesleyan message was couched seems archaic today. We must be bold to ask, then, how people experience divine grace today. And we must be open and sensitive in hearing what they have to say, for although we can describe the ways in which we and our forebears have experienced life before God, we cannot script the Holy Spirit. We can only ask, and expect to be surprised by the movement of grace.

In our sensitivity to the ways in which people experience the divine mystery today, however, we cannot sacrifice our own tradition's passionate concern that saving grace is more than a casual relationship. As we said at the beginning of this chapter, this understanding of the "way of salvation" is one of the great treasures of the Wesleyan heritage, and it demands cultural sensitivity as we try to express our faith in a multicultural age. What we are looking for is evidence of depth and of long-term commitment. We have been born again to life in Christ, and this is a relationship that "demands my soul, my life, my all" (Isaac Watts, in the *United Methodist Hymnal*, no. 299).

QUESTIONS FOR DISCUSSION

1. Which of the historic terms introduced in this chapter have you heard about before, and which are new to you? Such terms might include *prevenient grace, awakening, justification, assurance, sanctification,* and *entire sanctification.*
2. Can you identify points in your own experience that would answer to what earlier Methodists understood as *prevenient grace, justifying grace,* and *sanctifying grace*?
3. In what ways do you think your own religious experience differs from this historic Wesleyan pattern?
4. If you could understand your life on the analogy of a journey shown on a map, where would you say you are now on that journey, and what will be the destination of your journey?

CHAPTER 8

Holiness of Heart and Life: Sanctification

May the God of peace himself sanctify you entirely; and may your spirit and soul and body be kept sound and blameless at the coming of our Lord Jesus Christ.

(1 Thessalonians 5:23)

Introduction

The word "holy" and the concept of holiness in our pluralistic society bring a vast array of eclectic images and definitions: people that are holy, places that are holy, water that is holy, and scriptures or writings that are holy, just to name a few. **What determines whether something or someone is holy?** Is something holy simply because it is set apart for religious purposes? What is the process by which something or someone becomes holy? The greater ethical question is whether or not it is possible to become holy? How holy is holy?

For Wesleyan Christians, holiness is understood as describing God's own character or nature. **The biblical imperative of holiness cannot be neglected, if we are to be faithful to our Wesleyan heritage.** The doctrine of sanctification in itself is not the unique or exclusive theology of the Wesleyan tradition. **Sanctification has always been a central spiritual and theological concern of historic Christian faith.** In fact, the Christian faith itself was often expressed and illustrated in the past by telling the stories of Christian saints, those who had been sanctified. The saints offer us an image of a multicultural faith for a multicultural world, for the saints were women and men, and they reflect the breadth of the world's peoples and cultures. The saints reflect the glory and goodness of God: the image of a halo surrounding the head of a saint in traditional Christian art is an attempt to show that a saint reflects God's goodness in our world.

The Wesleyan tradition has been characterized by its emphasis on sanctification. The doctrine of Christian holiness ("sanctification" means "to make holy") has always been a hallmark of the Methodist movement. The fact that Wesleyans and Methodists sometimes had serious divisions over teachings about sanctification shows how important this doctrine has been for them. But the first thing we have to say about a Wesleyan understanding of sanctification is to say that for Wesley and the Wesleyan tradition, **sanctification**, like justification, **is by faith.**

Grace and Faith

Wesley's development of the notion of divine grace cooperating with the human will, or, as Randy Maddox calls it, Wesley's notion of "responsible" grace, maintains the implications of free will and prevenient grace against the teaching of irresistible grace.

Though **faith is the human response to grace**, it is important to reiterate that **faith is not a human possibility apart from God. Grace and faith are gifts of God through the Holy Spirit.** Faith is the appropriate way in which humans respond to the prevenient, justifying, and sanctifying grace of God. Human beings can and must be colaborers with God in the great work of redemption.

Holiness

The words "holiness" and "sanctification" are related, but have distinctive meanings. **"Holiness" refers to the presence or character of God reflected especially in the quality of human**

beings' moral and spiritual lives, while "sanctification" is the process by which human beings are made holy. Salvation involves not only deliverance from the penalty of sin, but it also includes healing from the debilitating effects of the sinful nature. **Holiness of heart and life is the goal of salvation**; for Wesley it included both inward and outward holiness, the former as the recovery of the image of God, and the latter understood as actual righteousness. It was Wesley's fundamental belief that anyone could become holy in this life through the work of God's transforming grace.

Holiness is a word Wesleyan Christians should claim and use without apology or hesitation. Holiness is more than the mere observation of regulations, commandments, and rules. It is the expectation that every believer can reflect the goodness of God, or in plain words, can lead a holy life. But how holy does God expect us to be? John Wesley consistently insisted that this measure of holiness is to love God with all our heart, soul, mind, and strength, and to love our neighbor. It is the rule of love; it is to love and desire what God loves. Love reigns in our life and not sin! He also made an interesting point: He contended that the divine objective in the life of holiness is in fact *happiness*, happiness that reflects the very nature or presence of God.

Moreover, the Wesleyan tradition insists that holiness is not an abnormal condition, but is rather a returning to the normal condition that God intended for human beings. Because of humanity's fallen nature, human beings have no inherent holiness. Holiness is derivative and dependent upon humanity's relationship to and with God. **Wesley believed that the grand theme running through the Bible is the loss and the recovery of the "image and likeness of God" in humanity.** In fact, he believed that the purpose of Methodism was to reform the church and the world through the proclaiming of scriptural holiness. Wesley said that the "great end of religion" was to renew our hearts in the image of God, and to repair that total loss of righteousness and true holiness. Any religion that does not attempt to answer this end Wesley called a "mere mockery of God." **Holiness is an essential component of salvation; it is not incidental or peripheral, but the primary theme of the Bible.** All the other motifs such as the *preferential option for the poor, the kingdom of God, the covenant of God* are not to be denied, but in the Wesleyan tradition should be seen as expressions of the overall theme of holiness.

Sanctification: Growth in Grace

The language of sanctification includes such terms as "holy," "holiness," "discipleship," "perfection," "perfect love," the "image of God," and "Christlikeness." The Bible explicitly demands that we are to be perfect, to be holy. It goes so far as to say that "God wants you to be holy" (1 Thessalonians 4:3*a* CEV). In Genesis 17:1, Abram is called to walk before Almighty God and be perfect. In Leviticus 11:44-45, 19:2, and 20:26, the people of God are repeatedly commanded to be holy. Finally, in the New Testament is the restated warrant "Be holy, for I am holy" (1 Peter 1:16 NKJV), and the warning to "pursue peace with everyone, and the holiness without which no one will see the Lord" (Hebrews 12:14*b*). If the term "perfect" offends our contemporaries, their complaint will have to be against Christ, who said "Be perfect, therefore, as your heavenly Father is perfect" (Matthew 5:48). "Perfect" appears here as a synonym for "holy." **Humanity's ultimate relationship with God and others is defined by holiness.**

Historically Methodists have described this process or growth in holiness as sanctification (from *sanctus*, "holy"). The *new birth* is the beginning of the new life in Christ, a life of growth in holiness. **It is the beginning of sanctifying grace.** Initial sanctification, the life-transforming power of grace that restores us to the image of God, begins at the moment of justification and regeneration (*new birth*). For Wesleyans, sanctification is not a joyless pursuit of good works or a grudging restraint from things we would really like to do, but know we should not. The fulfillment of the Great Commandment to love God with all our heart, soul, mind, and strength and our neighbor as ourselves, and the careful following of God's *moral law* (which preeminently includes the Ten Commandments) is an integral component of this process of *growth in grace*. The pursuit of sanctification is the pursuit of ultimate joy, and we come to love and desire that which God wills and loves. The kingdom of God is "righteousness and peace and joy in the Holy Spirit" (Romans 14:17*b*). **Wesley will not allow for an understanding of salvation and reconciliation that denies a real change or transformation of the person.** Included in his concept of salvation is the notion of healing from the disease and pollution of sin.

Imputed and Imparted Righteousness

The Reformation idea of "imputed righteousness" maintained that we are viewed as righteous because of the atoning work of Christ. "Justified and still a sinner" summarized a historic Reformation concept of justification, but this formula by itself was unacceptable to Wesley. "Imputed righteousness" implied only what Wesley called a "relative change," but **he insisted that what the Scripture requires is a change in character, and a change in the state of the relationship between God and humans.**

Here we encounter the debate that pitted "imputed righteousness" against "imparted righteousness": **Are we *declared* holy or actually *empowered to become* holy?**

Wesley argued that God does not simply declare us to be what we are not; God does not believe us righteous when we are unrighteous. **God not only *declares* us holy by granting pardon and forgiveness of sin, but actually *makes* us holy through the empowering, transforming presence of the Holy Spirit.** The imputed righteousness of Christ leads to the impartation of Christ's righteousness (and thus our sanctification), according to Wesley. Sanctifying grace transforms our will and our affections. We are enabled to become holy, the reign of sin is broken, and there is liberation from the tyranny of sin.

The Definition of Sin

But this raises the issue of how we understand the word "sin." Defined in a legal sense, "sin" is any deviation from the perfect will of

God, whether intentional or not. The power of sin is broken in the *new birth* and so believers are given power to avoid committing of voluntary sins. However, the grace given us is not an "inability" to sin, but is rather the power to overcome sinning. **To avoid misunderstanding, it is helpful to remember that Wesley argued that "sin," strictly defined, is a voluntary transgression of the known law of God.** It is not that the believer is unable to sin, but the believer is able to look at deliberate, willful sin and say, "no thank you" through the power of grace. Sanctification means that through the transformation of our will, our desire is to do what is right and to avoid what is evil.

The Bible employs the ethical meaning of sin when Christians are commanded to live without sin. Sin is not a thing—it is a relationship. **Sin is fundamentally self-centeredness; it is humanity's refusal to accept God as Creator and human beings as creatures, created for God's purpose.** It is the craving to worship self. A radical change is required, and what is necessary is a new humanity! "So if anyone is in Christ, there is a new creation: everything old has passed away; see, everything has become new!" (2 Corinthians 5:17). Human beings need to be converted from idolatrous self-sovereignty and self-sufficiency, back to God. New Testament language admonishes us to lay aside the old, corrupt self and be "renewed in the spirit of your minds, and to clothe yourselves with the new self, created according to the likeness of God in true righteousness and holiness" (Ephesians 4:23-24). Similarly, Jesus called us to deny ourselves (the old, corrupt self). Wesley continually made reference to sanctification as "having the mind of Christ" (Philippians 2:5, "Let this same mind [attitude] be in you that was in Christ Jesus").

Evangelical Repentance and Consecration

Because sin remains, even in believers, it is necessary for believers to repent. "Evangelical repentance" comes from faith and is the human response to divine grace. Evangelical repentance is not the same as repentance prior to justification. Repentance prior to justification is the result of convicting grace that awakens a need for the forgiveness of sin, and a sense of guilt and separation from

God. In evangelical repentance, the Christian remains conscious of the acceptance of God, and there is no guilt or condemnation. However, the Christian believer experiences a growing awareness that something inwardly is not right. **Though the acts of sin have been dealt with in conversion, there is the recognition of the inward nature of sin, the root of our sinful acts and attitudes.** Conviction returns in the life of the Christian and there is a discerning of the need for heart cleansing.

In his sermon "On Sin in Believers," John Wesley states that after the new birth there is a continuing presence of sin in the Christian. However, **sin no longer reigns**, and the Christian is no longer under the dominion of sin. Nonetheless, carnality is still a reality and there exists a conflict of flesh and spirit. **It is not a question of conscious, deliberate sin, but the relinquishment of self-sovereignty.** Simply put, the Christian's will is not fully subordinate to the will of God.

Wesleyan Christians often call upon believers to *renew* their commitment to Christ or to *rededicate* themselves to Christ. E. Stanley Jones reinforces this concept by insisting that conversion marks the introduction of a new life that brings "release from festering sins." The old life is subdued, but what is needed is surrender. This inward battle is a battle of motives, the mixed intentions of selfish, self-centeredness against the resolve to love God and others.

Wesley made an important distinction between justification and the beginning of sanctification. Justification is what God does **for us**, and the new birth and initial sanctification is what God does **in us**. The concurrent effect alongside justification is a radical change of heart, and the affection of the heart radically altered. It is grace that transforms and enables believers to "love God with all their heart, and to love their neighbor as themselves." Sanctification is an ethical transformation and assumes a real change.

Christian Perfection: Perfect Love

Be perfect, therefore, as your heavenly Father is perfect. (Matthew 5:48)

In postmodern society the notion of perfection may be offensive if not rightly explained and understood. However, it must be noted that the notion and the demand of perfection are biblical. First, Christian perfection is the divine intention of God. For Wesleyan Christians the Great Commandment is definitive: "You shall love the Lord your God with all your heart, and with all your soul, and with all your mind" (Matthew 22:37; cf. Mark 12:30, Luke 10:27). Along with this the Methodist and the Wesleyan tradition insists that Christian perfection also means the fulfillment of the second commandment: love of our neighbor. These are the factors that determine perfection.

Second, it is important to recall that Christian perfection is the result of divine empowerment: no human being can attain self-perfection! Biblical holiness is described in terms of love. **Love is the fulfilling of the law**. We need not get nervous with the term "perfection" if we avoid the implication of an absolute perfection, without flaw or need for improvement. Wesley stated that there exists "no perfection by degrees." In the biblical sense, then, "perfection" denotes a continual pursuit and a lifelong process and understood as something that fulfills or reaches its intended purpose. Perfection is the realization of the purpose for which God has called us—to love God with all our heart, mind, soul, and strength and to love others. As Søren Kierkegaard said, "Purity of heart is to will one thing—the good." Methodist missionary E. Stanley Jones referred to Christian perfection as a "full surrender." There is no Christian growth without the surrender of the will. A decision of the will determines one's actions.

Perfection in the biblical context is relational perfection and not moral or absolute perfection. It is not "sinless" perfection. **Christian perfection is the gift of divine grace, rather than the ability and resource of human effort.** Wesley insisted that it be defined as Christian perfection to denote the limitations and weaknesses of finite humanity. It is not perfection in fulfilling the letter of the law, but in fulfilling the spirit of the law (Romans 8:1-4; 13:8-10). In Wesley's understanding of holiness, Christians, being made free from sin, are also "made perfect in love." This he clearly defined not as freedom "from either ignorance or error...not from infirmities...nor from temptations," but freedom from "all outward sins...also from the sins of the heart." **Wesley made it clear that we are to look forward to being made perfect in love.**

Entire Sanctification

At this point it is important to clarify the term **"entire sancti-fication."** Justification deals with our forgiveness of sin, pardon, and reconciliation, and is a crisis experience—an instantaneous work of grace.

Regeneration, initial sanctification, and growth in grace are included under the rubric of sanctification. Entire sanctification denotes the sovereign reign of grace and the dominance of love in the life of the Christian. **Wesley stood in a long tradition of Christian spiritual writers who took sanctification to denote the completion of the Great Commandment that we love God with all our being.** Wesley equated entire sanctification with being filled with the Spirit and being made perfect in love. He insisted that entire sanctification involved a love that is incompatible with sin; it is an unmixed love that expels sin. According to Wesley, when love for God is the principle action, there can be no sin (again, in the strict sense in which he defined "sin"). The sanctified do not delib-erately transgress the law of love. Entire sanctification is the deliv-erance from original sin and from sin, properly so called. (Remember from chapter 6 that sin properly understood is defined as **a voluntary transgression of a known law of God**, involving a moral choice and responsibility in sinning.) If sin can be referred to as a "perversion of love," then **entire sanctification** can be under-stood as the fulfillment of the commandment to love God with all that we are: heart, mind, soul, and strength and others as ourselves.

Within the Wesleyan tradition there exists a range of views on the doctrine of entire sanctification. Some have argued that sanctification is *only* a progressive work, a growth in grace, and that entire sanctifica-tion comes at the moment of death (or thereafter). That is, sanctification denotes only a gradual growth in holiness. The problem inherent in a view of entire sanctification as process (only) is that it seems to limit God's power, and may reflect wariness about any claims that God's intention (perfect love) can in fact become a reality in this life.

The Wesleyan tradition in general has historically maintained that it is in fact possible to be entirely sanctified in this life. Wesley often asked: "Do you expect to be [i.e. look forward to being] made perfect in love in this life?" Because entire sanctification is a gift of divine grace, there is no reason why God cannot bring it about in this life. Wesley believed that entire sanctification itself occurred momentarily or in an instant of time. In his sermon on "The Repentance of Believers," **Wesley articulated the need for a second work of grace, for our Lord to speak to our hearts again, to speak the second time, "Be clean."**

A further nuance of the understanding of entire sanctification is characteristic of the Holiness tradition. In this tradition, the gift of perfect love is typically professed as the result of an instantaneous, "crisis" moment (similar to the crisis moment of conversion). Not only does this reflect Wesley's understanding that entire sanctification could occur in a moment of time in this life, but it also reflects the view that humans are *aware of* the moment when this occurs. This position also emphasizes and reaffirms that the crisis moment of "entire sanctification" is accomplished by God's grace through faith and not any works-righteousness on our part. One danger in this position is the tendency to believe that sanctification is a completed process and there is no need for further growth in perfection (a position that Wesley himself would not maintain). A more balanced perspective would hold that entire sanctification, as a momentary experience needs to be balanced with the need for continuing growth in Christian sanctity. When Wesley spoke of entire sanctification he was careful not to neglect the gradual growth and process that preceded it and followed it.

One further aspect of the contemporary debate centers around the issue of whether Wesley connected "entire sanctification" with the **"baptism of the Holy Spirit"** (Acts 2). This connection itself seems to imply a crisis experience, a second definite work of grace. The term "baptism of the Holy Spirit" was used by Wesley's assistant John Fletcher to describe entire sanctification. Although Wesley himself appears not to have used this particular term in his own writings, recent scholarship has begun to take note of early Methodists' (including John Wesley's) frequent use of Pentecost language to describe the culmination of sanctification.

Wesley's concern (and ours) should not be to place the emphasis on the *method* (crisis or process) by which a person is entirely sanctified, lest we fail to proclaim the possibility of entire sanctification and the pursuit of holiness of life. To be entirely (wholly) sanctified means that every part and aspect of life is sanctified. Nothing is withheld from God's rule. This should not be a matter of dispute for Wesleyan Christians.

Conclusion

When Mother Teresa of Calcutta died, the world saw a remarkable outpouring of affection for a simple Catholic woman who had given her life to work with the poorest of the poor in Calcutta. For all its spiritual blindness, the world seems to recognize saintliness—what we have called holiness in this chapter. The great gift of the Wesleyan tradition is not simply a doctrine or teaching about holiness or sanctification; the great gift that God has given is actual holiness on the part of women and men who have reflected the glory of God in our world. The terms and teaching our tradition uses are simply vehicles to express the experience of women and men. It is this actual holiness that will, in all likelihood, convict and convince our multicultural contemporary world of its need for divine grace. The imperative for us, then, is not only to be faithful in teaching the doctrine of sanctification, but it is the challenge of actually reflecting the splendor of God's glory—God's own holiness—in our world.

QUESTIONS FOR DISCUSSION

1. What are the distinctions and similarities between holiness and sanctification?
2. How is the doctrine of faith related to the doctrine of sanctification?
3. What is the distinction between imputed and imparted righteousness?
4. What changes take place through sanctification?
5. What is entire sanctification?
6. What would it mean to express a Wesleyan notion of holiness in a multicultural world?

CHAPTER 9

What's the Point
of Worship?

I was in the spirit on the Lord's day. (Revelation 1:10*a*)

Introduction

We have seen in chapter 5 that a pervasive sense of "the loss of the sacred" haunts contemporary life. A guest article in the *Washington Post* in the mid-1990s told the story of a woman's rekindled interest in Christianity after years of inactivity. She went from church to church in a quest for spirituality. She said she found discussions of activities, discussions about the Bible, notices of committee meetings, just about everything except what she was looking for. And what was it that she sought? In her own word, what she sought was "reverence," a sense of holy mystery. What a judgment on our churches! The "loss of the sacred" has come into the sanctuary. And this in a time when there is a hunger for the sacred in the multicultural world outside our doors (see chapter 5).

We must be careful in approaching this topic, for emotions run high on the subject of worship. We should be wary of quick fixes. A pastor of an inner-city United Methodist church in Oakland, California, once related to us the story of his congregation's long struggle for revitalization. After eight years of soul-searching and prayer, the congregation discovered renewed life and mission in its setting. Part of this renewal was a renewed sense of God's presence in worship. But the pastor expressed his frustration with visitors who come and see, for example, that the congregation is using bongos on

88

a particular Sunday, and conclude that if they just add bongos, their own congregations will experience a similar renewal. It's not going to happen, he says, without the searching and prayer. Be careful in considering this topic and heed his warning. Long-standing problems are seldom fixed with quick solutions.

The Sense of Divine Presence in Historic Worship

The point of historic Christian worship is **to convey a sense of divine presence**, indeed to usher believers into the presence of God. The story of the conversion of Prince Vladimir, whose baptism in A.D. 988 led to the conversion of Russia to Orthodox Christianity, illustrates this point. As a young man, Vladimir traveled throughout the world, and experienced a variety of religious traditions including Catholic Christianity and Islam. He entered the great Church of Holy Wisdom (*Hagia Sophia*) in Constantinople and was so awed by the rich beauty of its worship that he said, "I did not know whether I was in heaven or on earth."

In the Western (Catholic) Church in **the Middle Ages**, this sense of divine presence accompanied Christian participation in the holy sacraments of the church, perhaps especially the sacrament of Holy Communion (the Mass), where Catholic Christians believed Christ met them face-to-face. Crucifixes and other religious images, the use of incense and candles in churches, the singing of haunting chants, bodily movements such as making the sign of the cross or procession in the church, respect and even veneration for the "relics" or human remains of saintly people, the soaring architecture of medieval cathedrals: Each of these factors contributed a sense of divine presence to believers. Medieval Christians believed that the mysterious presence of God surrounded them, even in their everyday acts.

Although **the Protestant Reformation** came to question many of these devotional practices, Protestants cultivated a sense of **reverence for the Scriptures** and for the word of God as it was preached in the congregation. They also insisted that **the sacraments** of baptism and Holy Communion should be regarded with reverence, as places where humans encountered the presence of Christ. The worship of John Wesley's **Church of England**, expressed in its classic *Book of Common Prayer*, sought a "middle of the road" between Catholic and Reformed traditions of worship. Wesley loved the Prayer Book, and his affection for its reverent sense of worship bequeathed to Methodists the inheritance of ancient liturgical traditions of the Christian church.

The sense of divine presence in Protestant worship was strongly enhanced from the late 1600s by **the introduction of hymnody**. Although Lutherans had used hymns, some Protestants insisted on singing psalms only in public worship. The use of nonscriptural religious verse (hymns) gradually came to be accepted in the 1600s. Isaac Watts (1674–1748) championed the use of hymns in Protestant worship, and contributed hundreds of classic hymns still in use. With Watts, moreover, we see a transition from the third-person objectivity of older hymns to the vivid introduction of the first person (singular and plural). This had the effect of placing believers and congregation in direct dialogue with the divine, and although these hymns may strike us as old-fashioned, they bore a dramatic impact when first introduced into Protestant worship:

> When I survey the wondrous cross
> on which the Prince of Glory died,
> my richest gain I count but loss,
> and pour contempt on all my pride.
> (*United Methodist Hymnal*, no. 298)

John Wesley's brother Charles further developed this strain of hymnody, contributing thousands of hymns that likewise expressed the drama of divine-human encounter.

In the early 1800s, American Christians (black and white) sang simple, haunting **"spirituals"** (like "Wondrous Love"). After the Civil War, the widespread use of pianos and more sophisticated musical training enabled the rise of **"gospel" hymns,** such as those of Fanny Crosby or Thomas Dorsey, with their impressive shifts in dynamics (volume) and their elaborate use of scales and chord progressions to heighten emotional response.

In the evangelical tradition, it was not only hymns but also preaching that served to heighten the sense of divine presence in worship. One of the particular contributions of early Methodists to Christian worship was to insist that Christian preaching should express **a range of appropriate religious affections**. John Wesley gave explicit instructions on preaching in which he made the point that a preacher's manner of speech, gestures, and facial appearance should all contribute to the communication of the gospel. When preaching on sin and judgment, for example, the preacher's face should reflect genuine horror at sin and the thought of divine judgment. When speaking on the joys of heaven, the speaker's face should express profound joy at the thought of intimate, eternal fellowship with God and with God's saints. If a preacher were to do otherwise, for example, to preach on sin and judgment with a bland or uninterested facial expression, the preacher's expression would contradict the message of the sermon. The very manner of preaching was to express a sense of divine presence confronting sinners and believers in the message.

Moreover, as the Methodist tradition and the broader evangelical tradition developed, **the congregation itself increasingly played a role** in heightening the sense of divine presence in worship, **even during the sermon**. John Wesley himself described preaching in "periods," by which he meant brief, oral units of speech punctuated by a sharp "cadence," usually an emphasized word or phrase with two metrical beats. (For example, the expression "The Lord our God has called us . . ." where the phrase "called us" is accented as the cadence for this "period.") The sermon was divided into periods with these cadences forming a kind of flowing rhythm, and the cadences became points at which the congregation could respond to the preacher's message, increasing the sense of flow and rhythm. This "periodic" style of preaching can still be heard in Welsh evangelical preaching, in African American sermons, and in the sermons of Holiness and Pentecostal preachers. In African American churches, this periodic style was enhanced by the "call and response" manner of speaking characteristic of many African cultures. The effect was even more profound when the sermon itself began humbly and then rose to an emotional crescendo, with congregational responses growing in intensity along with the preacher's voice. This historic manner of evangelical preaching offered a deep sense of divine presence running through the whole assembly.

The effect of **all these elements together**—a sacramental sense of divine presence, reverence for the Scriptures and preaching, the use of emotionally moving hymns, emotive preaching that called for congregational response—was to heighten the sense of divine presence in historic Protestant worship, especially (as we have described it here) in the evangelical tradition. We should not downplay the importance of sacramental celebration in the evangelical tradition either: American camp meetings originated in Presbyterian sacramental celebrations, and typically culminated in the celebration of the Love Feast or Holy Communion (in some cases, both).

The Loss of the Sacred in the Sanctuary

We urged caution at the beginning of this chapter, because issues about worship raise high emotions today. One of the reasons for this is **a widespread sense that something is not right**, especially in the worship of "mainline" or "oldline" Protestant churches in the United States, and nowhere more clearly than in United Methodist worship. Much of what is said in this section is directed particularly toward The United Methodist Church, and may not be as relevant to other Wesleyan denominations. There are two ways in which the "loss of the sacred" (see chapter 5) has affected worship in Methodist churches: the sense of divine presence has been diminished both in (a) liturgical, sacramental celebration and in (b) the evangelical ethos that focused on the call for conversion and sanctification. Let us consider both of these challenges to contemporary worship.

In the first place, **Methodist worship in many cases seems to have lost the sense of mystery, reverence, and sacred presence** associated with traditional liturgical and sacramental celebration. Some have argued that this more liturgical piety was never strong in Methodist circles (because of the prevalence of revivalistic forms of worship), but accounts of Methodist services from the 1700s and 1800s are full of terms that suggest this sense of God's presence: "reverence," "solemnity," "awe," "religious sensibility." Even where written liturgies were not used by congregations, preachers continued to use the hallowed language of the older prayer books. Charles Wesley's hymns express the depth of this reverential piety. Of the Lord's Supper, he wrote,

> How can spirits heavenward rise,
> by earthly matter fed,
> drink herewith divine supplies and eat immortal bread?
> Ask the Father's wisdom how:
> Christ who did the means ordain;
> angels round our altars bow to search it out, in vain.
> (*United Methodist Hymnal*, no. 627)

Who could possibly read (or sing!) these words with any degree of understanding and fail to perceive the immense mystery of Christ's presence in the Supper?

But today's services, even Holy Communion services, seem too often to be characterized by a kind of **casualness that suggests that participants do not really sense themselves to be in the presence of a holy mystery**. Perhaps it was the fact that Methodists said (and eventually believed) that all of life is sacred, and that Sunday morning should not be regarded as being more sacred or religious than any other part of life. But this idea seems to have gone terribly wrong, and now seems to haunt us with the possibility that worship should seem as devoid of God's presence as any other aspect of modern life. Of course, no one factor can account for this; it is surely the pervasive influence of a secular worldview that has now come into the holiest of holy places and suggests that our most sacred rituals are merely shells, forms, merely words and symbolic acts, void of divine presence.

In the second place, Methodist worship seems also to have lost the sense of direct divine-human encounter in the call for repentance, conversion, and sanctification. Part of the drama of an evangelical event was the sense that someone might be "awakened" or converted or "sanctified" in that very meeting. The great drama of salvation was to be enacted in this very place. Heaven would rejoice over a single sinner who repented and turned to God. We have seen above how hymns, preaching, and the responses of the congregation all contributed to the sense of divine presence in evangelical worship.

Methodist worship today largely **lacks this dramatic call for immediate personal repentance and conversion**. It is not just that the "altar call" or invitation to discipleship no longer appears at the end of the service; what is more critical is that contemporary Methodists seldom have occasions (such as camp meetings or revivals) when an entire event aims at the inculcation of repentance, faith, and holiness. Evangelicals are sometimes inclined to blame this on Methodists' use of more formal, liturgical styles of worship, but as we have seen above, the sense of reverence and holiness in liturgical worship seems as absent as the drama of repentance and conversion. The truth is that the "loss of the sacred" appears to have affected all of our historic forms of worship.

Lacking the sense of holy, reverential mystery in liturgical celebration, and lacking the dramatic call for immediate, personal repentance and conversion, Methodist worship can become a dull ritual of reciting traditional prayers, halfheartedly singing hymns, and talking **about** religion, without the expectation that anything religiously significant will actually happen. Nothing could be duller, and nothing could be so distant from the central point of Christian worship, to usher believers into the presence of the living God.

Conclusion

A number of **new options** have opened up in the area of Christian worship in recent years. "Contemporary worship" involving praise music, "seeker services" that try to present the gospel in a pagan-friendly atmosphere, and new efforts at hymnody and creative imagery to express the faith have been tried by Christians. Serious attention has been given to the broadening of traditional worship to accommodate and celebrate the diversity of cultures that are brought together around the Christian table. Multiculturalism, we might say, has come to church. Our intent in this conclusion is not to be prescriptive, but to suggest some guidelines for the appropriation of a Wesleyan vision of worship in our new settings. We have five particular observations.

First, a Wesleyan vision of worship must stress **the centrality of the presence of God** in our worship. Whatever form our worship takes—traditional, liturgical, revivalistic, "contemporary," or worship adapted to particular cultural traditions—worship must bring women and men into the presence of the living God. If we have forgotten what reverence means, we must relearn it. There is no easy prescription for how we convey a sense of divine presence, but we shall know it when we encounter it. Our facial expressions, our tone of voice, our bodily gestures, the manner in which we handle the Bible or communion elements, everything about us will communicate reverence in the divine presence. Perhaps the best way to begin, as our friend in Oakland suggested, is with intense and prolonged prayer in preparation for this encounter with the divine.

Second, a Wesleyan vision of worship would seek **a balance of liturgical and evangelical experience of the divine presence**. John Wesley loved the Prayer Book and the liturgical worship it conveyed. He also preached itinerantly, sometimes in the open air, and presided over religious meetings with intensely emotional outpourings. Both the liturgical and the evangelical senses of the divine presence had a place. These were not necessarily blended together: Methodist Sunday worship was often more liturgical, and Methodist camp meetings and later revival services were intensely evangelical and dramatic in their calls for repentance, conversion, and holiness. Wesleyan spirituality can be described as a "sacramental evangelicalism," and we should cultivate the sense of divine presence in both of these traditions of worship.

A third element in a Wesleyan vision for worship would be **attention to the corporate dimension of worship**. By this we mean that worship cannot be the expression of an individual; it must somehow express the "consensus," literally the "feeling together" of a whole

95

community. Paying attention to the corporate dimension in worship might mean a choice to use the words agreed to by one's Church rather than improvising or making up one's own words in worship. Paying attention to the corporate dimension of worship would mean that worship would engage the whole people of God, rather than being the act of a single performer or a small group of leaders. Paying attention to the corporate dimension of worship might mean asking members of the congregation to write or at least review prayers for use in services, so that they are not simply imposed upon the congregation by the will of a single worship planner.

A fourth element in a Wesleyan vision of worship would be **the faithful adaptation of worship to particular cultures** and constituencies. Wesley's sermon on a Catholic Spirit made it clear that particular manners of worship were among the "opinions" on which Christians could differ; they did not constitute the "essentials" on which Christians must insist. This was consistent with an Article of Religion in Wesley's Church, taken over by the Methodists, which states that

> it is not necessary that rites and ceremonies should in all places be the same, or exactly alike, for they have been always different, and may be changed according to the diversity of countries, times, and men's manners, so that [or, "so long as"] nothing be ordained against God's Word. (22nd Article of Religion)

This Article, we should note, goes on to give a stern warning against persons who would violate the orders of worship that had been agreed to by churches, but the intent of the statement is to affirm that liturgical customs may be changed according to "the diversity of countries, times, and men's manners," that is, what we would call cultures. A Wesleyan vision of worship, then, would exhibit sensitivity to the variety of cultures in a congregation or locality, and would incorporate those cultural traditions into the community's experience.

A fifth and final element in a Wesleyan vision of worship would be the guiding notion that **worship should express the life of holiness**. In our worship, we state what we believe to be the ultimate, the final reality in the universe. We sing our praise to the eternal triune God, joining other Christians throughout the world, and through all the ages, in an immense variety of cultures and tongues, "with angels and archangels and all the company of heaven." This great company of saints is already a multicultural company; we have only to invite others to join us in the ceaseless chorus of praise.

QUESTIONS FOR DISCUSSION

1. What did Saint John the Divine mean when he said that he was "in the spirit on the Lord's day" (Rev. 1:10)?
2. How do the worship experiences in your congregation convey a sense of reverence in God's presence?
3. How do the worship experiences in your congregation convey a sense of the drama of the call for personal repentance, conversion, and holiness?
4. How can we worship so that we and others perceive God's divine presence in our midst?
5. How can worship in your congregation appeal to people of highly different cultural backgrounds?

CHAPTER 10

Christian Behavior in a World Where "Anything Goes"

Submit yourselves therefore to God. Resist the devil, and he will flee from you. Draw near to God, and he will draw near to you. Cleanse your hands, you sinners, and purify your hearts, you double-minded. (James 4:7-8)

Introduction

One of the strongest challenges that contemporary society offers to historic Christian faith lies in the area of Christian behavior or morality. Compared to traditional societies even as recently as the period of World War II, it would appear that "anything goes" (or, "anything goes between consenting adults"). What is particularly difficult in this new situation is that the larger society can no longer offer the kind of moral guidance that it once offered. Public schools are not teaching the Ten Commandments. If Christians are to be formed in a distinctly Christian morality, then, only our religious communities will be able to bring about that formation. But sometimes, even churches seem powerless in the face of the moral ambiguity of wider society.

Part of the distinct genius of the Wesleyan movement was its unique manner of moral formation. By making clear their moral expectations, by organizing Christians into small groups where these moral expectations were personally affirmed and voluntarily enforced, and by regular preaching and teaching that enhanced these moral expectations, Methodists developed highly effective ways of moral formation. The success of such groups as Alcoholics Anonymous and other Twelve Step groups shows the continuing moral power of methods that Methodists pioneered. Methodists were great at "behavior modification."

Perhaps most important, the Wesleyan movement did not see moral formation as a strictly individual matter, nor did it understand moral formation to be a matter of simply following rules. Moral formation **was linked to the Wesleyan insistence on sanctification** (chapters 7 and 8) and the belief that divine grace can transform our "wills." That is, grace can change what we desire, what we love and what we detest, so that morality becomes an expression of what we and God together truly desire.

Historic Christian and Wesleyan Teachings

The **early Christian movement** had high moral expectations for its followers. In many cases, early Christians believed that if a person committed a sin that offended or brought disrepute on the Christian community, that person had to be cut off from fellowship, never to return. This is probably the meaning of the long and complicated sentence that takes up verses 4 through 6 of the sixth chapter of Hebrews. The fact of persecution and the temptation to save one's life by offering incense to honor the Roman gods (or the Roman emperor) presented a severe challenge to the church. Even by the 100s A.D. the possibility of restoration or "reconciliation" to the congregation was discussed, and some congregations came to allow a one-time reconciliation after **public confession** ("with tears"), a period of **segregation** from the church, and then a **formal reconciliation** with a Christian bishop. In some cases, penitents were required to go to the Roman prisons and beg forgiveness of fellow Christians who were awaiting execution.

Although the practice of public confession persisted for centuries, by the early Middle Ages Christian communities had come to allow for reconciliation by **private confession** to a bishop or a priest. The term "reconciliation" bears important meaning here: It implies that a believer who had committed a serious sin (such as breaking one of the Ten Commandments) had cut herself or himself off from communion with the Christian church by their acts. The church then acted to "reconcile" such penitents to its community. The church might announce or proclaim Christ's forgiveness to those who earnestly repented (John 20:23), but the church's primary act was an act of reconciling sinners to its own communion. Although catechesis (training in the faith) was irregularly practiced in the Middle Ages, when it was practiced it involved **instruction in the Commandments** and teaching about the Creed and such prayers as the "Our Father" (the Lord's Prayer) and the "Hail Mary."

By the 1200s the church regarded penance (including confession) and reconciliation as a sacrament. The Catholic Church in the late Middle Ages (the 1300s and 1400s) developed **a concern to discern the intentions of penitents**, that is, to try to discern whether a person was truly penitent before proclaiming absolution (Christ's forgiveness) and reconciliation. In order to discern a person's motives, a priest would often ask the person to perform a penitential act (a "**penance**") such as returning stolen goods or saying traditional prayers. The priest could pronounce forgiveness and reconciliation based on the person's willingness to perform these acts as a sign of the person's sincere intent. (It is important to know that actually performing the penitential act was not the grounds of reconciliation; this is why Catholics maintained that their penitential discipline did not amount to "works righteousness.") In some cases, the church came to allow for the substitution of one penitential act for another—this was referred to as an "**indulgence**." Although these penitential practices may seem alien to Protestants, they show that the medieval church was concerned not only to teach moral behavior, but also to enforce it as well, and with a concern for the intentions behind particular acts.

The **Protestant Reformation** reacted against some of these medieval means of moral formation. **Luther**'s "95 Theses" were originally directed against abuses of the system of penances and indulgences, but although he eventually came to reject the use of indulgences altogether, he continued to hear private confessions. Lutheran Catechisms (such as the Luther "Small Catechism") included instruction in the Commandments, but Lutheran theology stressed the manner in which Christian faith frees us from slavish "bondage" to the Law. Lutherans believed that Christian moral behavior would flow from faith in Christ, although Lutherans did not stress or emphasize the proclamation of the moral law.

The **Reformed tradition** (the tradition of Zwingli and Calvin, of Congregationalists and Presbyterians) differed with Lutherans on this point. Although Reformed Christians believed that the "ceremonial law" of the Old Testament was no longer binding on Christians, they believed that the "**moral law**," especially the Ten Commandments, called for precise obedience. The historic Reformed insistence on Sabbath observance, for example, expresses this belief in the morally binding character of the law.

In the 1600s, Reformed congregations developed a particular manner of enforcing moral **discipline**. Richard Baxter's classic account of *The Reformed Pastor* (1656), one of John Wesley's favorite works, describes the manner in which the Reformed clergy should visit every family in the church quarterly. The pastor was to inquire about the family members' manner of life. Reformed Christians were encouraged to keep diaries in which they recorded their spiritual struggles, and these could be shared with the pastor when he visited. If the pastor was convinced that the members had not committed any offense that would bring disrepute on the community, he issued a **ticket** that admitted the member to the congregation's quarterly celebration of communion. This practice of "**fencing**" communion (the term historically used to describe it) was designed to ensure that the community gathered at Eucharist had exercised moral responsibility for its members.

The Wesleyan Contribution

Although Wesley's Church of England as a whole had not embraced the Reformed pattern of moral discipline, many Anglican priests had attempted to enforce discipline in this manner. Moreover, the last decades of the 1600s had seen the flourishing of "religious societies" within the Anglican Church that did indeed develop covenants between small groups of believers and provided a regular means of holding each other accountable for moral behavior. It is clear that John Wesley was influenced by these "religious societies," and in fact his little circle of Oxford Methodists seems to have been precisely this kind of group.

As the Methodist movement developed, Methodists used three means of moral formation. First, Methodists made their moral expectations clear in a common document called the "**General Rules.**" Drawn up in 1743, the General Rules were a kind of contract laying out expectations for moral life that were conditions for continuation as a member of a Methodist society (and later, a "class" when the societies were subdivided). They specify moral expectations in three areas:

> to avoid evil of all kinds (and several very specific matters are mentioned, including working on the Lord's Day, and the use of "spirituous" or distilled beverages);

> to do good of every kind (such as feeding the hungry, clothing the naked, and visiting the sick and those in prison); and

> "attending upon the ordinances of God" (prayer, scripture study, the Lord's Supper, fasting, and "Christian Conference" or conversation).

The General Rules have been a part of every Methodist *Book of Discipline*, and are still a doctrinal standard in the United Methodist Church, the African Methodist Episcopal Church, the African Methodist Episcopal Zion Church, and the Christian Methodist Episcopal Church.

A second element linked closely to this pattern of Wesleyan moral formation was **moral accountability in small, voluntary groups of believers**. Early Methodists were gathered into societies, which were subsequently subdivided into classes. The class was expected to meet weekly, and the subject of the meeting was to ask members if they had kept the General Rules. David Lowes Watson, whose Duke dissertation on these meetings has been published as *The Early Methodist Class Meeting*, points out that the distinct genius of these meetings lay in their sense of moral and spiritual accountability: They were not primarily groups for Bible study or for sharing spiritual experiences. The focus was on accountability to the Rules that everyone had voluntarily agreed to keep by becoming a member of a class. In recent years, Watson has been instrumental in renewing the use of classes in what United Methodists have come to call "Covenant Discipleship."

A third and critical element of Wesleyan moral formation was simply **moral preaching**, that is, preaching on specific topics of moral interest. Methodists were known for their preaching against slavery, on behalf of temperance in the use of alcohol, and address-ing any number of social and personal moral issues. Methodist preaching, when it was faithful to the Wesleyan tradition, attempted to inspire believers with the challenge of sanctification and the power and comfort of the Holy Spirit to face all trials and tempta-tions. Methodist preaching linked morality to the "way of salva-tion" (chapter 7) and the quest for entire sanctification (chapter 8). Moreover, Methodist preaching was expected to reinforce the moral expectations that had been laid out in the General Rules and (eventually) in the *Discipline*.

Wesleyan Morality in an Age When "Anything Goes"

What would it mean to follow the Wesleyan pattern of moral formation today. We would suggest three things. First, **Wesleyan Christians need to make clear their moral expectations**. In a world where "anything goes," it is especially important to make clear our own expectations. This does not need to be a matter of per-sonal opinions: Christian churches (including the United Methodist Church) have specific statements of the moral expectations that they have historically taught. The Ten Commandments and the Great Commandment must be explained consistently to children and adults alike, and they must be explained not on the level of one more set of opinions available in society. They must be explained as moral expectations to which our churches have agreed. Moreover, the moral teachings of such documents as the Methodist "General Rules" can challenge contemporary Wesleyan Christians with the distinct ethical heritage of the Wesleyan movement.

Second, **Wesleyan Christians can rediscover the power of moral discipline in small, voluntary groups**. The real key to moral discipline in the Wesleyan movement was the understanding that members had entered into a voluntary covenant with each other, and that once having entered into this covenant, they could expect members of their class to hold them accountable for their behavior. The contemporary model of Covenant Discipleship suggests that Christians form small groups, then formulate a covenant that expresses their expectations. These covenants should be specific enough to be asked about from week to week, and they should be challenging, that is, they should involve some matters that participants are not in fact consistently doing. Once the covenant has been formulated, members of the group should sign and date it. Subsequent group meetings may involve prayer or devotional Bible study, but should hold members consistently accountable for the behaviors to which they have agreed. Even if the pattern of Covenant Discipleship is not adopted, other groups such as men's and women's groups, youth groups, and Sunday school classes can ask from time to time if they should formulate specific goals to which they can hold each other accountable.

Third, **preachers in Wesleyan and Methodist churches can be encouraged to address a variety of moral issues**, making clear their church's consensus about morality and linking this to the quest for Christian holiness. Preaching must never become "moralism," that is, simply preaching on moral issues as if we believed that humans by themselves had the power to do or to be good. But Christian preaching needs to address far more than controversial contemporary issues: It must make clear the whole range of Christian ethical expectations. In a Wesleyan context, it should make clear the missional expectations of congregations and other groups. Above all, moral preaching should offer inspiration, the sustaining power of divine grace to transform ourselves and our communities.

Conclusion

Historic Christian moral teachings may stand in sharp contrast with a multicultural world in which it appears that "anything goes."

On the other hand, a multicultural world may call us to recognize that some of the moral practices we have taken as essentially Christian in the past have simply been expressions of our own cultural traditions rather than essential and long-standing parts of Christian morality. When in the 1970s, for example, a friend decided to keep her maiden name after marriage, an acquaintance commented that this was "unscriptural." How could it be unscriptural if surnames were not developed until the late Middle Ages? How could it be un-Christian if in fact Christians almost never acknowledged surnames in baptism? It is too easy to suppose that moral practices that seem common to us must be biblical and Christian. One challenge of a multicultural world to Christian morality is the challenge of discovering what is, in fact, consistently part of the Christian moral tradition, and what is simply an artifact of human culture.

Within the scope of Methodist churches, one unfortunate consequence of the liberal-conservative division that has affected our churches has been its tendency to divide moral issues. Conservative Christians, at least in the past, have tended to emphasize such issues of personal morality as sexual purity and abstinence from alcohol and tobacco. Liberal Christians have often addressed broader social issues with great passion. We shall address a Wesleyan vision for social reform in chapter 11, but let us note here that a Wesleyan moral vision should include personal and social transformation. Christ calls us to holiness, personal and social holiness, and offers us grace to pursue that vision of holiness.

QUESTIONS FOR DISCUSSION

1. In what ways does your congregation make clear its moral expectations for Christians? How often are the Ten Commandments taught and explained?
2. Have you ever experienced formation in a voluntary community (this does not have to be limited to church groups: it might include Twelve Step programs, or even weight-reduction programs that involve the format of a voluntary agreement to which members hold each other accountable)?

3. If you were to form a voluntary small group for moral formation, what expectations would you suggest that the group take up and hold members accountable for?
4. How can Christian preaching sustain and inspire moral life, while not becoming "moralistic"?
5. What contributions could persons of widely different cultural and ethnic backgrounds make to our understanding of Christian morality?

CHAPTER 11

What "New Creation"?: Christian Social Responsibility

Religion that is pure and undefiled before God, the Father, is this: to care for orphans and widows in their distress, and to keep oneself unstained by the world. (James 1:27)

Introduction

Christians are called to follow Christ's example of **compassion.** The Wesleyan revival movement in England involved significant efforts for aid to persons caught up in the social upheaval brought about by the Industrial Revolution. John Wesley, followed by faithful American Methodists, championed the cause of the abolition of slavery, and later Methodists engaged in the struggle for the prohibition of beverage alcohol in the United States. Methodists took up the plight of women and children and persons caught in tragedies brought about by the expansion of American industrialism, and advocated public assistance for each of these. These acts of social responsibility were inspired by the vision of a sanctified society: God's **new creation** was to come on earth, and Christians were to be in the vanguard of that great cause.

But **what "new creation"?** Can the Christian vision for social transformation be identified with a political program for social reform? Or, does it simply mean the transformations brought about by individuals as they are converted to Christian faith? Can Christians be significantly involved in social transformation without surrendering their essential or core identity as Christians? This chapter examines the ways in which Christians are called to social responsibility in a contemporary multicultural society, and the ways in which the Wesleyan heritage may be a resource for Christian engagement with the contemporary world.

Compassion, Charity, Church, and State

The **earliest Christians** were known for their compassion. The Roman official Pliny, writing to the Emperor Trajan in the early 100s A.D. used the term *heteria* to describe Christian communities. This word had been used in the Roman world to describe "clubs" or "societies" in which members took responsibility for each other, including providing funeral expenses for members and providing for the upkeep of members' families after their deaths. In other words, this outside observer thought of the Christians as a community of people committed to caring for each other. His impression concurs with the ways in which Christians thought of themselves, as it appears from the epistle to James (1:27), the Acts of the Apostles (Acts 2:46-47; 6:1), and other early Christian literature.

Through the **Middle Ages** Christians developed institutions for the relief of the poor and the needy (including orphanages), and institutions for the care of the sick and dying (especially hospitals and hospices). Early in the Middle Ages these institutions were founded and sustained by monks and nuns, whose religious orders were committed to such relief efforts. With the rise of European cities from the 1100s A.D., dioceses under the leadership of a bishop often became the focal point for Christian relief efforts. Medieval Christians came to view the poor with particular reverence, believing that Christ himself was poor, and that the poor on earth bear the most literal image of Christ. We "store up treasures in heaven," they believed, by giving our earthly treasures to the poor.

The **Protestant Reformation** brought about a revolution in Christian treatment of social ills almost accidentally. In dissolving the monasteries and older diocesan structures that had provided for the relief of the poor and the upkeep of institutions for the poor and

108

the sick, Protestant states found themselves without means of administering Christian relief efforts. Increasingly, in the late 1500s and early 1600s, relief efforts came to be administered by political states, or by the combined efforts of political and church officers. Since churches were established by the state in almost all Protestant countries, church-state cooperation in relief efforts was a natural expectation. The distant germ of the modern welfare state lay in this process of nationalization of relief efforts on the part of Protestant nations.

But the degree of relief offered in most Protestant countries was quite meager. In response to this situation, German **pietists**, who led a powerful spiritual revival within European Protestantism in the 1600s and 1700s, began to develop voluntary charitable institutions. For example, pietist leader August Hermann Francke built a series of relief and educational institutions, including a famous orphanage in Halle. The compassion of German pietists became widely known and influenced English leaders such as George Whitefield and John Wesley.

The Wesleyan Vision of Christian Compassion

John Wesley did believe that the **state's involvement** in relief efforts was appropriate, and he called for compliance with such state-sponsored efforts on behalf of needy persons as the Elizabethan "Poor Law." But Wesley was also influenced by reading he had done in Anglican and Catholic spiritual writers (such as Thomas à Kempis) that suggested the need for voluntary relief, and he was inspired by the relief and educational efforts of pietists. He came to believe, as we shall see, that voluntary societies of Christians were called to assist and educate the poor.

It is important to recognize that by the early decades of John Wesley's life, the social situation in England had changed radically by the advent of the **Industrial Revolution**. The Industrial Revolution brought about a significant shift in population, with persons moving from the countryside to new industrial cities (and industrial suburbs of older cities), where they hoped to find work. It is clear that this displaced population accounted for much of the constituency of the early Methodist movement. Kingswood, for example, where Wesley regularly preached near Bristol, was a new industrial suburb populated by "colliers" (i.e., coal miners). Leaders of the Church of England were aware of the challenges to its traditional parishes brought about by this population shift and attempted to form some new parishes, but the masses moving to the cities were largely without spiritual or social help.

Wesley's decision in 1739 to act as a traveling or itinerant evangelist meant that **he had chosen to meet England's new poor on their own turf**. What Wesley brought to the poor was the gospel, "good news to the poor." But he knew the poor by traveling and even living among them. He would later reject the argument that the poor were poor because they were "idle" or lazy— Wesley had simply lived among the poor long enough to know their stories, and their stories showed the falsehood of this claim. Increasingly, the work of the Methodist movement came to embrace face-to-face aid to the poor in Wesley's England.

The **General Rules**, which served as a covenant or contract among early Methodists, required members of Methodist societies to ask each other every week if they had done good to all people, including:

> To their bodies, of the ability which God giveth, by giving food to the hungry, by clothing the naked, by visiting or helping them that are sick or in prison.

> To their souls, by instructing, reproving, or exhorting all we have any intercourse with; trampling under foot that enthusiastic doctrine that "we are not to do good unless our hearts be free to it."

> By doing good, especially to them that are of the household of faith or groaning so to be; employing them preferably to others; buying one of another, helping each other in business, and so much the more because the world will love its own and them only.

> By all possible diligence and frugality, that the gospel be not blamed. (From Ted A. Campbell, *Methodist Doctrine: The Essentials* [Nashville: Abingdon Press, 1999], p. 114)

These rules show the character of charity and compassion in the early Methodist movement. Methodists were engaged directly with the poor, and took responsibility for the poor, especially poor persons in their own societies ("them that are of the household of faith"). It became a movement of the poor helping the poor: As soon as a person was enrolled in a class, despite their own poverty, that person was expected to give weekly for the relief of the poor.

Although these efforts on behalf of the poor were carried out within the context of the voluntary Methodist societies or classes, Wesley's engagement with the poor led him to **engagement with some broader social issues** in his time. As we have mentioned above, Wesley advocated compliance with the existing "Poor Law" in England, which provided for limited assistance for the poor through public work houses (the proverbial "poor house"). His "Thoughts on the Present Scarcity of Provisions" (1773) offered an analysis of broader economic conditions in his age, showing why these conditions had forced persons into poverty. In the later years of his life, Wesley became seriously involved in the effort for the eradication of slavery. A letter written two weeks before his death encouraged antislavery crusader William Wilberforce's efforts to secure parliamentary action against the slave trade and the institution of slavery.

Wesley's social vision was, above all, **a vision of social holiness**. The world was eventually to reflect God's justice, and Christians were called to the task of making the world a place fit for holiness. This was linked to Wesley's vision of the end of time. He was convinced that Christ would return soon, and Christian engagement with the world's social conditions, as well as Christian evangelism (chapter 12), were both signs of the coming reign of Christ.

Three Challenges to the Wesleyan Vision

As the Wesleyan movement has grown, its powerful social vision was challenged in many ways. Although revivalism had been tied to social reform efforts in America through the middle of the 1800s, the Wesleyan vision clashed with a powerful under-standing of the reign of Christ that became popular after the U.S. Civil War. The **premillennial** outlook of American evangelicals in this period emphasized Christ's return to remove the church from the earth for a thousand years. This outlook had the effect of dis-engaging evangelical Christians from the social conditions of the world around them. Many Methodist and holiness leaders came under the influence of premillennial theology, and they came to think of Christian faith as a matter of individual piety to prepare persons for leaving this world. Concrete engagement with the poor or with the social ills of their age were not seen as being central to the gospel, as Wesley and earlier Methodists had seen them.

Shortly after the rise of the premillennial theology, the older Wesleyan vision was also challenged by the rise of the **social gospel**. The social gospel was a movement for the relief of the con-ditions of workers, women, and children in the growing cities of the United States at the beginning of the twentieth century. Although many early advocates of the social gospel espoused the evangelical outlook of nineteenth century Protestants, the movement came to be dominated by the liberal theologies of that age. The movement turned increasingly to the social sciences for its models of Christian engagement with the social world. As a result of the popular pre-millennial theology in America and the rise of the social gospel, **social engagement was increasingly divorced from evangelical theology** and evangelistic appeal, especially in Methodist churches (the movement did not influence holiness and conservative Wesleyan denominations as decisively). Moreover, the social gospel paved the way for social activism at the level of national denomi-national structures rather than direct, local involvement with needy persons, as had been the case in the earlier Wesleyan model. We should note at this point that the division of the Salvation Army from Methodists in the 1800s (originally from the British Methodist New Connexion) was a tragedy for all Wesleyans, for the Salvation Army has been able to sustain the direct contact with the needy that was so central to Wesley's own vision.

A further challenge came in the form of **liberation praxis** in the later twentieth century. Liberation praxis urged the use of

Marxist models of social analysis as a ground for Christian engagement with social issues, and encouraged Christians to engage the deeper causes of poverty and discrimination embedded in social and economic systems. Although the term "liberation theology" has been prominent, "liberation praxis" conveys more the sense that Christian engagement should involve a twofold activity of engagement and reflection (the "praxis" model). Although the fall of Soviet communism in the 1980s had the effect of discrediting Marxist ideas, advocates of liberation praxis insisted that they were committed only to Marxist social analysis, not to Marxist political solutions. Liberation praxis challenged older Christian notions of charity and voluntary acts of compassion in its concern with the larger economic and social structures that could only be engaged at the level of social and political protest.

Like the social gospel movement, liberation praxis had a far greater influence on Methodist churches than on holiness or conservative Wesleyan denominations. This fact presented a particularly challenging situation with respect to liberation praxis, which advocated concrete identification with ("solidarity with") the poor. But since the Methodist churches had come to be identified with the middle classes in the United States and elsewhere, how could Methodists live out the idea of identification with the poor? The approach taken by Argentinian Methodist theologian José Miguez Bonino in the last two decades bears particular interest here. Professor Bonino came to realize that the Holiness and Pentecostal churches of South America represented the poor in his continent much more consistently than did the Methodists. His praxis reflection has continued to use Marxist and other forms of social analysis, but he has increasingly engaged the Holiness and Pentecostal family of churches in dialogue with Methodists as reflecting the concerns of "Christ's poor."

Conclusion

What would it mean to live out a Wesleyan vision of social holiness in today's multicultural society? We would suggest four elements of a renewed Wesleyan vision today. First, **a Wesleyan social vision calls for direct encounter with suffering persons**. In the Wesleyan model, there can be no antiseptic treatment of the poor by simply giving donations to organizations. A worker at the Jubilee Center in Washington, D.C., was once queried about what to do if asked for a handout by a homeless man. She did not tell whether she would give him money, but her response was challenging and unexpected. "First," she said, "you should ask him his name." The poor and the needy are not statistics; they are real human beings, with real stories. Whatever practical course we take, we must not avoid the direct, eye-to-eye contact that brings suffering into our own reality. It is foundational for a Wesleyan vision of social transformation.

Second, **a Wesleyan social vision would call for understanding the reasons for poverty and suffering**. Wesley tried to understand why people were becoming poor in eighteenth-century England. We should try to understand as well. Shifting economies, population shifts from one region to another, and rapidly changing systems of governmental and private relief are all factors in understanding the human need we may encounter. Similarly, an understanding of the crises of contemporary medicine and the new challenges that medical science may pose will also help our understanding of the roots of suffering in our society. Likewise, it might be important to ask how advances in information technology contribute to social problems and open up new areas for employment.

Third, **a Wesleyan social vision would seek appropriate private and public means of addressing social conditions**. Wesley attempted to influence local officials to enforce the legal options for relief of the poor. There are conditions that today are of such a magnitude that only concerted effort, perhaps on the part of a whole society, can address them. In particular, we need to be well informed about our own churches' national and international efforts for the relief of social conditions. For United Methodists, for example, this might mean becoming better informed about the work of the General Board of Church and Society and the efforts of the United Methodist Commission on Relief (UMCOR). But on the other hand, there are always local expressions of social problems, and in response to them, Christians can never simply surrender social service to governmental or public agencies or even denominational agencies. We have to ask carefully what we can do in our localities, and what we must support at larger and public levels.

Finally, **a Wesleyan social vision must hold to the central vision of social holiness.** Those with whom we participate in service do not have to hold our views, but Wesleyans must be faithful to the gospel as we have received it. This does not mean that hungry persons must listen to sermons before being fed, but it means that Christian groups must be quite clear and uncompromising in the grounds of their social service. It is not just a "great society" we seek; it is a world redeemed by Christ and made holy by divine grace. We are called to communicate this vision of social transformation in the multicultural world in which we find ourselves today.

QUESTIONS FOR DISCUSSION

1. What do you believe are the most pressing social issues in your region or area?
2. How do these issues reflect broader social issues in today's world?
3. What is your congregation, your regional church structure (annual conference) and your denomination doing to respond to these issues?
4. How does your response, or your denomination's response, reflect a vision of social holiness?
5. What could you and your congregation do to live out a Wesleyan vision of social transformation in today's world in your own setting?
6. How can you be in direct contact with needy persons in your locality?

CHAPTER 12

Mission in a Multicultural Society

Go therefore and make disciples of all nations, baptizing them in the name of the Father and of the Son and of the Holy Spirit, and teaching them to obey everything that I have commanded you. (Matthew 28:19-20)

Introduction

Is the world—the multicultural world in which we live today—still our parish, as John Wesley's world was his parish? Wesley confidently proclaimed the gospel in a turbulent time of social upheaval, cultural transition, political corruption, and a shifting worldview, similar to the rapidly changing paradigms of the twenty-first century. As we noted in chapter 1, **a multicultural society confronts us with the ambiguity of relativism, the notion that there is no objective standard of right or wrong. At the same time (chapter 5), the postmodern world shows a growing interest in and openness to spiritual things.** This rising spiritual consciousness is a quest for meaning. It is an attempt to wrestle with the emptiness of contemporary secular culture. The marginalization of religion, and the opinion that faith is not a proper subject for public life or discourse, has added to this emptiness. The image of religious life has been distorted and warped by contemporary, popular culture and confused by religious pluralism.

Therefore, the challenge facing the church is to live out the

gospel with integrity, without denigrating other religious beliefs. What we bring to the dialogue of religious pluralism is the proclamation of God's decisive act of overcoming sin and death through the incarnation, death, and resurrection of Jesus Christ. The proclamation of the gospel is not an option for Wesleyan Christians. The biblical mandate is undeniable and crucial. The imperative of Christ is that the gospel be proclaimed to the ends of the earth. The duty of Christians and churches is the intentional witnessing and proclaiming of the gospel of Jesus Christ. We seek a world redeemed by Christ and made holy by divine grace (chapter 11). The inescapable responsibility of the church is to share the "way of salvation." The doctrines on the authority of Scripture (chapter 2), the finality of Christ (chapter 4), fallen humanity (chapter 6), and the universal availability of grace (chapter 6) mandate the evangelistic task and the church's call to mission.

The Gospel and Culture

Wesleyan Christians must attempt to understand the mission of the church, the role of culture, and the command to proclaim the gospel together. When we think of multicultural ministry, the church is immediately confronted with issues of affirming cultural identity without either absolutism (seen in the ugly form of imperialism), or the total relativism of all culture and the unguarded syncretism to which relativism can lead.

Culture is a given in the sense that it is impossible to find a human community without culture. In *Who Comes in the Name of the Lord*, Methodist theologian Harold J. Recinos defines culture as "an always changing, socially acquired system, which provides explanation about individual identity and social life." Culture provides meaning for interpreting experience and for generating behavior that allows persons to successfully adapt to their physical and social environment.

Therefore, religion is always adapting to culture. The religious and social rituals are powerful tools of cultural reality. They are symbolic images and representations that embody a system of belief, that constitute solidarity, and inculcate social and political beliefs and values. It would be naive not to admit or realize that our own religious beliefs and Christian identity are viewed through our own culturally biased worldviews. **Every understanding of religion comes by way of some cultural venue.** Paul on Mars Hill engages and uses the Athenian culture to proclaim the authentic message of the gospel (see chapter 1). The articulation of the gospel is not culture-free. However, by its very nature the gospel calls into question and critiques all cultures.

Multiculturalism holds out the possibility that there can be unity without uniformity. Perhaps our greatest problem has been distinguishing Jesus' promise of oneness from our own concepts of oneness and unity. **Cultural "hegemony" refers to the situation where only one way of thinking, one way of seeing, is allowed and accepted.** Historians have noted only in the last few decades how the traditional skewing of history has led to textbooks filled with the exclusive viewpoints and experiences of Western white males. Breaking that hegemony has led to the rediscovery of African American history, women's history, Native American, and Latino American history—experiences that were often viewed as worthless by the power structures. But the gospel is counterhegemonic, and offers an alternative that is not determined from the dominant culture or center, but from the margins and periphery. God's self-disclosure is revealed in culture, and it is this cultural particularity that confronts and challenges us. The gospel critiques the structures and systems of present society to provide the possibility for a new formation of society—the reign of God. Through Jesus Christ the whole world is being reconciled to God, and the world is being brought into the reign and kingdom of God.

The Mission of the Church

To have clarity about the mission of the church, we must have clarity about the gospel. The gospel begins with the assertion that we are living in an aberration of God's creation (see chapter 6).

The heart of the gospel is the incarnational message of Jesus Christ, a particular rabbi and particular person who entered historical time. He is the Word made flesh, who calls us to repentance, and to be reconciled with God and with one another. We are to help usher in the kingdom of God. We are to help prepare for God's shalom (peace), which offers universal justice and peace to all, and to assure "[God's] kingdom come [and God's] will be done, on earth as it is in heaven" (Matthew 6:10).

In one sense the church does not *have* **a mission, it is** *on* **a mission** derived from the redemptive mission of the Triune God: the mission of God as revealed through Jesus Christ and the active presence of the Holy Spirit in the world. Mission constitutes the very being of the church, the mission of Jesus Christ to reconcile the world to God, the Father. **The church is sent into the world to extend and prolong the incarnation through its mission** *in* **the world.** The church is called to live in active obedience and faithful discipleship, while waiting for the fullness of shalom.

The Holy Spirit enables us to engage in mission, to witness to the reality of the gospel, and to work in the world. Faithful discipleship demands that it is essential to live life in the way God purposes the world should be, according to the life of Jesus Christ. Faithful discipleship affirms in the ambiguity of the present the certainty of the future; the fullness of the reign of God which is to come.

To proclaim Christ crucified and risen is to proclaim possibility and change. The heart and center of Christian faith is the resurrection of the crucified one through the power of the Holy Spirit. The Resurrection initiates something new: a new life from God based on reconciliation with God; a new life that is stronger than sin and death. Jesus' resurrection life is life giving, and is the entrance into kingdom life here and now. **The church is to articulate and exemplify the Resurrection by its community of love, inclusivity, forgiveness, and acceptance.** The purpose of the local church is to be a community of disciples living in loving fellowship that, through word and deed, witnesses to the reality of God's saving event in Jesus Christ.

119

The Church as the Body of Christ

God has chosen to use the church as an instrument of God's mission in the world. The church is the means of evangelism, not the goal or source. **The major biblical image of the church is of the reconciled Body of Christ.** Paul's theology of the church is the most developed in the Scriptures. In 1 Corinthians 12:12-13, he states: "For just as the body is one and has many members, and all the members of the body, though many, are one body, so it is with Christ. For in the one Spirit we were all baptized into one body—Jews or Greeks, slaves or free—and we were all made to drink of one Spirit." This image of a human body is applied to the church. **We are together Christ's body, the physical expression of who Jesus is *in* the world.**

It is fundamental that all believers, whatever their background, culture, language, or gender, are incorporated into one body. Human distinctions of inequality or oppression are broken down. Any concept of the church that sees the church as Christ's body must be inclusive. For Christ, as head of the church, has made his body an inclusive one for all who would believe. The vision of heaven is of "a great multitude which no one could number, from every nation, from all tribes and peoples and tongues" (Revelation 7:9, adapted). Setting up walls that divide and separate can be a form of spiritual rebellion. It undoes the reconciling work of Jesus on the cross and abandons the central element that makes a true church of Christ—being for the world. Therefore, the missional intention of the church is in its *sentness* as a servant for the world. "As you have sent me into the world, so I have sent them into the world" (John 17:18).

The mission of the church and the kingdom of God are not identical. By proclaiming and advancing Christ's rule in a particular time, place, and culture, the church aims at *realizing* (making real) the Kingdom by witnessing to it. The church has the responsibility to live out its mission as the anticipatory sign of the reign of the Kingdom and the rule of the King. The church must be a transforming presence, as the servant of the Kingdom. However, the church itself is not the final goal of mission. When the

Kingdom comes in fullness we won't need conventional church institutions: Christ did not give his life for an institution but for the world.

It is paramount in dealing with diversity and inclusivity that **the church not fall victim to enculturation and surrender the gospel, adapting it to cultural convenience**. This is particularly dicey in multicutural settings where on the one hand, we want to celebrate our cultural diversity and find a unity in our differences. And on the other hand, we want to prevent the church from adjusting the gospel to please and serve whatever the world dictates as desirable and important.

The church is to be more than a reflection of what is happening in the world. It is not to concede the gospel to culture and its influence; it is to be an alternative and distinctive culture. At the same time, the church in the United States must remember that evangelism and conversion are not synonymous with the adoption of Western culture.

Inculturation

Jesus calls the church to be different from the world in its values and lifestyle, even while not separating itself from the people of the world. The gospel requires various cultural expressions to transmit the good news of God's love and transforming grace through Jesus Christ. This is a powerful combination—living *in* the world, but not *of* the world. Wesley used the metaphors of salt and light in conveying the responsibility of the evangelistic task. Wesley's logic is illustrated in his comments on Matthew 5:13-15. According to Wesley believers are to season others, and to allow their holiness to shine as the light of God.

God is at work in the world through the church, the Body of Christ. The church, a people not in charge of its own destiny, is committed to God's destiny. The church makes choices, takes action, orders lives, and with temerity pronounces that it is the will of God. The church does not live in opposition to the world. It is to live active *in* the world (again, think of Paul on Mars Hill). These

121

images of permeation, pervasion, and insertion all suggest that the church must not withdraw from or attempt to control the world, but to transform the world from within.

The task of the church is to serve and not be preoccupied with internal concerns and survival while the pluralistic world of massive suffering and oppression is ignored. Institutional maintenance is not a good enough reason or motivator for persons to reach out to others and share the good news. There must be a balance in meeting the internal needs of the church and the needs of the world to be a credible witness of the gospel. It must practice what it preaches.

The church must preach and present the gospel of Jesus Christ with integrity. By its own transforming encounter with Jesus Christ, the church is empowered and compelled for the evangelistic task. Mission is expressed in what God has done for us in the person of Jesus Christ. The Incarnation is the consistent thread that runs throughout the Scriptures. Essential to this incarnational understanding is the cross and the atoning death of Jesus. Jesus instructs us to "take up our cross and follow him." Therefore, Wesley's missiology and evangelism are a call to a radical discipleship. It is a fundamental stance and strategy of incarnational servanthood by way of the cross. It is holiness lived out in faithful acts of love.

Wesley's definition of the church, as the spiritual community of God's people, shifted the focus from the church as institution to the church as community. **The church does not exist for itself, but exists for the world.** The community of faith is a community of transformed humanity that reforms and transforms the structures of human society. On such terms, the more we grow in holiness, the more we will give our lives in service to others—in the church and in the world.

Renewal of Mission and Evangelism

We need a renewed vision for mission and evangelism. God has brought the world to us in our evangelical pursuit—our contemporary multicultural world is an unparalleled opportunity to evangelize and usher in the kingdom of God. The conventional view of evangelism is usually proclamation or visitation, which is often dismissed as activism and pragmatism at its worst. Certainly these are part of evangelism and mission, but not the whole. **Evangelism must include nurture and discipleship that results in a missiological endeavor to transform the world into the kingdom of God.** The Wesleyan message of proclaiming justification by faith and holy living is a dynamic for mission and renewal. It was in the context of renewal that Wesley found and proclaimed the demand for scriptural holiness, and that his understanding of the assurance of faith, that would empower this movement, was hammered out.

Faith, justice, and righteousness have not been established. Brokenness and heartache still abound. No church, whatever its location, can presume to be done with its mission and evangelistic task. What is lacking is not only a vision to see the need, but also a compelling and energizing passion to embrace the need as the call of Christ.

Passion is the natural result of the fullness of faith and the active presence of grace through the Holy Spirit. It is the love of God shed abroad in our hearts by the Holy Spirit (Romans 5:5). God's love for us, and our love for God and others becomes the motivating factor of evangelistic effort. If love reigns in our hearts and lives then our lives will be given to the evangelistic and redemptive task. It is not an obligatory and perfunctory duty, but passion—a passion to do and be what God desires us to be.

Compassion Evangelism

The Bible is explicit in conveying the notion that holiness is inextricably bound together in relationships and patterns of conduct with the whole world. **The reconciliation and transformation of the person is the beginning of the transformation of the whole earth.** To transform and restore society requires a radical change of the human heart.

123

Wesley's articulation of holiness, while emphasizing the necessity of personal holiness, did not allow for the privatization and individualization of the purpose of full salvation. To be a Christian meant being an active participant in the transformation of the nation, and the assurance of individual salvation. Wesley could not conceive of personal holiness that did not manifest itself in social holiness. Christian witness is not an argument to be won, but an act of genuine caring and compassion for other people, a tangible concern for their welfare.

Wesley consistently maintained that Christians, being made free from sin, are also "made perfect in love." It was *freedom to love God and all humanity* with a pure and whole heart. Led to faith by grace, we are naturally led to do the "works of mercy" by the whole-hearted (pure) love of God and neighbor, which has grown within us. **Mercy is the immediate response to human need.** It is feeding the hungry, clothing the naked, healing the sick, and sheltering the homeless. Such acts and ministries of compassion will always be needed in this sinful world, and our faith will compel us to do acts of mercy. Wesley sought to help the poor through organizing clinics, homes for unwed mothers, credit unions, and schools. **Evangelism must be the Word made flesh; it must include not only preaching and deliverance from sin and freedom from guilt, but also justice for the oppressed and the dismantling of systemic evil.** Systemic evil is the result of institutions and structures that create and perpetuate policies, attitudes, and programs of racism, poverty, oppression, sexism, and the like. The grace of God must not only transform individuals, but must also be the agent of reform for society as a whole.

Though there appears to be a resurgence of social, compassionate evangelism, it is paramount that the gospel not be truncated. The trajectory of evangelism must include discipleship and accountability that results in mature Christian living. Sanctification, **faith working in love,** is the goal of our mission and message. Wesley's social concern was concretely rooted in the essentials of Christian faith. He held that **transforming grace would effect the redemption of fallen humanity, and would also redeem and renew society**. To be connected to God, is to be connected with God's people. There is conveyed in this connection a tension between conversion on a personal, individual level and conversion on a communal, social one.

Conclusion

For John Wesley there was no division between personal holiness and engagement in social holiness. In fact, he said that to hear the distress of the afflicted requires a concrete response to human affliction in whatever form. It is necessary to avoid a linear view of evangelism. It is not a one-dimensional message and proclamation of grace. There must be a comprehension of the wholeness of the gospel as grace active in mission to avoid a truncated gospel. It is in the proclaiming of the gospel that the Holy Spirit enables evangelism, and that the vitality for evangelism is maintained and perpetuated. The vitality and strength of renewal should be measured by the incarnation: Are people more Christlike in their personal piety and more loving in relationships? Do they have a closer walk with God, which issues in a passion to lead others to that faith and that life? Just as God took on human flesh and came into the world in Jesus Christ, we must leave the safety of our sanctuaries and institutions, and enter into the world to do the work that Christ did. Our mission and evangelistic task is still to make disciples of all nations, to convert individuals and societies through the proclamation and living out of the gospel. To be committed to the multicultural world in which we now live as our own parish and mission is to be faithful to our Wesleyan heritage.

QUESTIONS

1. Do you agree that there is a rising spiritual consciousness? How might this present an opportunity for evangelism?
2. How do we live out the gospel with integrity?
3. Is religion always adapting to culture? What are some contemporary examples of the enculturation of the church?
4. What is the difference between mission and evangelism? Or are they synonymous?
5. What does it mean that the evangelistic task must be "the Word made flesh"?

CHAPTER 13

Marketplace Christianity:
Living Authentically

*I appeal to you therefore, brothers and sisters, by the mercies of
God, to present your bodies as a living sacrifice, holy and accept-
able to God, which is your spiritual worship.* (Romans 12:1)

Introduction

In chapter 1, we learned that we are to **contend for the faith**
that was handed down to us in every area of life. We are called to
proclaim the gospel faithfully in the midst of our multicultural
world. But it is easy for Christians to be discouraged. Does the
gospel of Christ really make any difference in the world? In a
world of tragedy, racism, violence, and poverty, with a church on
almost every street corner, where is the connection of personal faith
in Christ and the qualitative change and transformation of society?

We seem to live in a time when religion is marginalized and
trivialized, intentionally omitted from public and professional life.
Popular culture enmeshed in a consumeristic philosophy and materialistic values seems to have warped and distorted the image of
religious life. Christianity is portrayed in the news and entertainment media as nonintellectual, comic, and bordering on fanaticism.
Religion typically is not given authority or respect. Faith and belief
can be ridiculed, dismissed as nonessential and irrelevant to contemporary life.

The gospel of our age often seems to Christians to be a gospel
of self-expression and the relentless expressions of individuality.

The only good news it seems to offer is that we are free enough to choose whatever we want. The good life becomes a supermarket of desires. What we call freedom often becomes a form of inward tyranny. As we go about fulfilling our needs and asserting our rights we live like strangers to one another. For its part, the church often becomes one more drive-up, consumer-oriented organization. We miss completely the biblical mandate and emphasis of salvation as a process of spiritual maturity within the church, and the corresponding responsibility to participate in God's redemptive mission *in* the world.

Consumerism and the Gospel

As we have seen from the beginning of this study, we live in a time of relativism, where there seem to be no absolutes and people believe that truth changes over time. We are left to ourselves to decide what is right and wrong. We are encouraged to go with whatever truth works for us. This postmodern, materialistic culture is all about free choice and a variety of options. Therefore, consumerism offers a variety of options and possibilities to give significance and purpose to life. However, there are not a variety of options for the Christian. **Truth, morality, and a way of life are derived from the authority of the Scriptures** (review chapter 2). The gospel of Christ transcends time and culture. The answer Christians bring to our postmodern world is their faithful living out of the gospel.

The values of society, the philosophy of the marketplace, and the overall consumeristic culture invade and shape our worldview. In a book entitled *Consumer Rites: The Buying and Selling of American Holidays* (Princeton, N.J.: Princeton University Press, 1995), Leigh Eric Schmidt shows us how Christianity has been intentionally redefined by the commercial culture to provide a foundation for a consumerist gospel. Consumerism's purpose is to promote a gospel of prosperity and abundance. When this is uncritically adopted, spirituality and faith are at the least affected by, and at the worst determined by, the

127

dominant consumer culture. God is treated as a consumer item. The church is seen as a spiritual supermarket where we shop to get our personal needs met—a place where we go to get and not to give. When we need to deal with the hurts, disappointments, and pains of life, we call on God. When circumstances improve we take back control of our lives, and we inform God that we can handle it from here.

Consumerism and materialism shapes our worldview and affects our spirituality. Consumerism's primary aim and persuasion is personal satisfaction. Its promise is to make people happy and comfortable, to feel good about their experience. It is a philosophy and a way of living that exalts the subjective, prizing the tangible and the immediate. It is a lifestyle of instant gratification and the tyranny of credit card debt. It is all about what you can experience now! Now is all that matters—no waiting, fast foods, ATMs, instant credit. We can have it now and pay later. It is a world of little restraint and a lack of patience. Consumerism places great value on and in things. Individuals are encouraged to do whatever it takes to get ahead. As Madison Avenue retorts, "you are worth it." We lose the focus on the eternal realities that require moral accountability in this life. The message is "buy it, it will make you feel good; it will make you happy. It will give meaning and add fulfillment to your life; it will change your life." **Consumerism is all about this world, not the things of God**—it is a grave danger to feed the self-centered, sinful nature, the me-first philosophy.

Consumerism is secular hope and temporary happiness. **Consumerism holds out to us material goods and service as a means and a promise for significance, hope, and happiness.** Hope is placed in and built upon the accumulation of material objects (things). Our real hope has been hijacked! The one who has the most toys wins? We buy things we don't need, with money we don't have, to impress people we don't like.

Happiness is a legitimate desire. But John Wesley equated holiness with happiness and warned that there can be no real happiness apart from God. Consumerism is not a sustainable way of life. It is a fable world and everyone does not live happily ever after. Jesus directs our attention to the priority of life. We are to "seek first the kingdom of God." Jesus then reminds and promises that all the other necessities and needs of life, will be added according to this priority (Matthew 6:33).

The inherent problem of consumerism and accommodation, and the extremes of seeker-friendly churches and the church growth movement, is doctrinal suicide at the expense of making people comfortable. The intention is not to be disparaging or negative about the megachurch phenomenon and movement, but to urge caution in regard to the danger of reinforcing a gospel that is consumer driven and convenience oriented. **However, the philosophy that we do not want to make people uncomfortable flies in the face of the gospel that is intended to be transformational.** We must avoid presenting religion as another consumer item, and Christianity as one brand among many slick products.

A Christian Worldview and Authentic Living

How we live in the world depends in large measure on how we think about the world. **For Christians it is essential to think about the ways in which life in this world can be lived because of God, and for God.** What is your comprehensive view of life? Today, religion and faith rarely challenge the assumptions of modern culture, and lifestyles are more defined by the culture than by the gospel of Jesus Christ. We are to challenge and critique the world in which we live by our Christian perspective. The Christian's worldview must not be determined and developed from the news media or the entertainment industry. The worldview of the Christian is God's view. **The basic question is how does a person live successfully and authentically as a Christian in an unchristian world?** Can a Wesleyan ethos (way of life) be developed and shaped in accordance with the Wesleyan essentials we have discussed?

In chapter 12 the church was defined as a countercultural structure that aims to influence the world by being something the world is not and can never be. The church is a people who are not their own, but the Body of Christ *in* the world, fleshing out the redemptive and reconciling love of God. **So it becomes necessary to ask,**

129

where is the church on Monday, or any other day of the week?
How do you take your faith to work, to school, and into the myriad of social interactions and political activities?

The Wesleyan Christian cannot ignore the ethical content of
conversion. Inconsistent Christian conduct discredits the gospel.
Wesleyan Christians cannot acquiesce to a standard of living and
lifestyle that is indistinguishable from the world. Wesleyan
Christians must avoid the temptation to compartmentalize life into
sacred and secular issues, or the division of personal and social
ethics. The world wants to know if Christianity is reliable. Is
Christianity credible? What should Christian discipleship (living)
look like in the marketplace when lived out against the background
of the consumer culture and materialism? **If the gospel is to be
effective, it must be *heard* in ways that can alter the experience
of the hearers, and it must be *seen* in a way that will open their
eyes to authentic Christian living.**

Many claim to have a relationship with Jesus Christ, and that
they have made a personal commitment to God. However, when it
comes to living out their convictions in faithfulness in marriage, in
integrity and honesty in business and professional ethics, and the
disciplined use of money, time, and leisure, their believing seems to
make little difference in real life. **A person's public life and persona is seen totally divided from the events or realities of their
private life.** Life is compartmentalized into public and private identities. This vitiates the concept of Christian conversion. The biblical
reality of grace is that something is supposed to change—the believer is to be a new creation.

What does it mean to be a public Christian? Does confessing the lordship of Jesus Christ have any meaning or impact on the
job? What does the Holy Spirit and authentic Christian living have
to do with medicine, the arts, law, computer programming, banking, real estate, and retail sales? Jesus is the Lord over all of the different facets of life and the whole of creation (Colossians 1:15-23).
By public Christian, we do not mean wearing a label or parading
our righteousness. Wesleyan Christians are committed to the
proclamation of the good news of Jesus Christ. You cannot be a
private or isolated Christian. **The Wesleyan paradigm is that**

grace received must be grace shared. It is at this point Wesleyan Christians are challenged with the reality that there is no holiness that is not social holiness. We are called to bless the lives of others as God has blessed our lives through Christ. It is a social ethic that demands moral responsibility and solidarity with those who are oppressed by injustice, racism, sexism, and poverty. It is to understand that we are forgiven so that we might forgive, accepted that we might accept, and loved that we might love.

When our lives are graced by the love of God through the saving act of Jesus Christ and the power of the Holy Spirit, that love compels us to love others through social reform and compassionate involvement. We are to be salt and light in the world, agents of change that proclaim the kingdom of God is here, and to live that proclamation as a present reality. This can be as simple as feeding the hungry or taking a stand against policies and institutions that marginalize and victimize people, disregarding human rights. We can convince people of the reality of a loving God only as we who bear the name of this God as Christians love authentically all the people of the world.

At the heart of Wesleyan essentials lies the concept of a personally assimilated faith. How do we help people and encourage them to lead upright, godly lives based on the truth of the Word of God? In a postmodern world we must meet people where they are and approach their world in practical, creative, and challenging ways. The United Methodist *Discipline*, in articulating "Our Theological Task," stipulates that the church (and by extension each Christian) is "called to identify the needs of individuals and of society and to address those needs out of the resources of Christian faith."

A Christian Worldview and Sanctifying Grace

Through sanctifying grace the hearts of believers are motivated by love to share the gospel, and through prevenient grace unbelievers' hearts are prepared to receive the gospel. Sanctifying grace radically alters the affection of the believer toward God and others. The "real" change in the lives of believers is the effective love of God shed abroad in their hearts. The actual creation of love in the heart is the result of faith. **This divinely given love is the evidence of genuine Christianity.** Wesley contended that the living out of the Christian experience and relationship is **faith active in love,** loving acts of mercy and compassion. Wesley consistently maintained that Christians, being made free from sin, are also "made perfect in love." He described this freedom as a freedom to love God and all humanity with a pure and whole heart. **Sanctifying grace affects not only spiritual transformation, but the moral transformation of life as well.** Further, sanctifying grace has both personal and social dimensions. Human love is empowered by God's love for all humanity. All Christian activity grows out of the life of holiness and love. The holy life requires sacramental living; living in such a way that we recognize the sacred amid the secular. Seeing God at work in all the areas of living avoids a division of the secular and sacred, and the compartmentalizing of life.

In a world that often seems to lack moral bearings, it is essential to stress individual and social transformation by divine grace. Grace enables and requires responsible action. The understanding of righteousness among most evangelicals has become almost synonymous with personal piety. Personal morality too often is associated with the negative aspects of "holiness." To be "righteous" is to avoid the commonly understood sins of personal behavior. This definition has unfortunately defined Christianity by what one does not do, rather than by any positive identifiable morality, let alone social responsibility. From its inception, a historic Wesleyan ethos has stressed moral responsibility and avoidance of specific evils, such as alcohol, tobacco, and profaning the Lord's name. However, the gospel challenge to oppression and injustice has from the very beginning engaged the Wesleyan movement in the struggle to eradicate slavery and racism, the civil rights movement, and in a broad sense, human rights in general. In his "Thoughts Upon Slavery," Wesley expressed his belief in the God-given right to liberty, human freedom. Wesley insisted upon this right for all persons, and the denial of human rights is not justifiable for institutional or individual gain. The good life, a livable life, must be offered to all human beings.

The Hebrew and Greek words translated in the English Bible by the word "righteousness" could just as accurately be translated in terms of "justice." The righteousness of God so often referred to in Romans, for instance, describes not simply a world where individuals refrain from personal sins, but also a world in which the structures of society are shaped to promote the ideals of the kingdom of God.

In his sermon on "The Scripture Way of Salvation," Wesley comments that in the progressive work of sanctification "we are more and more dead to sin, we are more and more alive to God." As we grow in grace it is necessary to abstain from the appearance of all evil, and to take every opportunity for doing good works. In order to make Christianity credible in the world, and biblical truth relevant to the needs of individuals and the whole of society, Christians must be sensitive to the hurts, needs, and concerns of individuals. They must create and model a community of faithful and obedient disciples. Christians are to be a living testimony of the transforming grace of God in the world. The church is not a hiding place for those who merely want to be known as Christians. It is a rallying place for those who are Christians. The church is the Body of Christ on earth. As Jesus, the incarnate Son of God walked among people, so the church walks among all of humanity. Being salt and light *in* the world causes us to think differently about justice, sexism, racism, inclusivity, equality, poverty, and wealth.

A Christian Worldview and Love Fulfilling the Law

The gospel calls us to reevaluate our relational responsibility toward each other and our stewardship of the world's resources and of life itself. It shows the love of God, and extends the hand of God to a needy world. It lifts up the fallen, comforts the lonely, ministers to destitute and needy, and confronts arrogant and cruel social systems and government institutions that victimize and oppress others. Christianity operates from a different perspective. It is a commitment to the obedience of God's purpose as revealed through the Word. It is faithfulness to God and accountability to the standards of God.

Our worldview derived from the Christian faith will encounter the social structures, dynamics, and relationships that crush and oppress others. The whole of theology and Christian duty, according to Wesley, is no more or less than love fulfilling the law. A working definition of Christian perfection is the fulfillment of the dual commandment of love: love for God and love for others. Proclaiming and living out the love of God puts us in daily contact with people in pain who need that love expressed in very concrete and practical forms. As the apostle John exhorts, "How does God's love abide in anyone who has the world's goods and sees a brother or sister in need and yet refuses help? Little children, let us love, not in word or speech, but in truth and action" (1 John 3:17-18). Social response must be intentional or it will never happen. The problems of racism, unemployment, poor education, poverty, and shattered relationships and families must be addressed by the grace of God that transforms not only individuals but societies as well. We must practice what we preach, a faith actively and tangibly touching others.

In Wesley's mind this religion of love was the remedy for the maladies of the world. He commented that, "this is the religion we long to see established in the world." Every Wesleyan Christian, for whom faith is a dynamic reality, is moved to love—**faith active in love**. Mission, then, must include meeting human need, and fleshing out the love of Christ in our actions. The visible and dramatic realization of love in the everyday world is the only proof that there is a God who is inclusive love. The imitation of God is the concrete response of those who hear the distress of the afflicted. Jesus reminds us, "By this everyone will know that you are my disciples, if you have love for one another" (John 13:35).

Focusing on love gave form and substance to the doctrine of holiness. Wesley continually remarked that God had thrust him out to raise a holy people who could make a difference only as "faith working by love" made them alive and able. Love of our neighbor was for Wesley a near synonym for perfect love, and could be known only in service to that neighbor. We are fully human only in relation to others, in community, when love rules our hearts. We can only truly love others in conjunction with our love for God. The evidence of holiness is not a withdrawal from society or the world, but a life filled with the social fruits of love.

Conclusion

The lordship of Christ is to be proclaimed in all the realms of life. He is Lord of all, or he is not Lord at all. Religious life as revealed in the Bible is not separated from daily life. It is a commitment to follow Christ in all things. Are we, as the Body of Christ a living witness to the integrity of the gospel? "As the Father has sent me, so I send you" (John 20:21). We cannot compromise the message of the gospel. It is the message of the cross. The cross challenges us to live authentic lives, lives of love and compassion. It requires sacrifice and serving; our conduct must match our convictions and confession. We are to be willing witnesses to the truth as revealed in Jesus Christ, and validate and exemplify that truth in reckless, unconditional love. It is a costly discipleship. Dietrich Bonhoeffer wrote in his book *The Cost of Discipleship* that the call of Christ is a call "to come and die." In accordance with Romans 12:2 we are not to be conformed to the world or squeezed into its mold. We are to be transformed by the renewing of our minds. This is our reasonable worship to God and service to humanity. It is necessary to insert a word of caution that we do not over react and condemn the material world. Or that we instill guilt because of the things a person has and owns through honest effort, hard work, and the grace of God. God created the world and announced that it was good—what we are condemning is unrestrained materialism and out of control consumerism. The biblical admonition is to use the material world properly and not let it control you.

Paul proclaimed the gospel on Mars Hill. John Wesley proclaimed the gospel in the streets of Britain's Industrial Revolution. The Lord has not called us to Mars Hill or to eighteenth-century Bristol. To be faithful to Paul and John Wesley and our foremothers

135

and forefathers in the faith, **to be faithful to Christ our savior, we must proclaim the gospel in the world in which we have been placed**. In this study series, we examined the multicultural society in which we have been placed, just as Paul tried to understand the Hellenistic world in which he had been placed, and John Wesley tried to understand the eighteenth-century world in which he had been placed. We are called to be open to our contemporaries. We are called to be relentlessly faithful to Christ. **We are called in the midst of our multicultural world "to contend for the faith that was once for all entrusted to the saints"** (Jude 3).

QUESTIONS FOR DISCUSSION

1. How would you interpret "contending for the faith" in contemporary life?
2. Is consumerism a religion? Is church in danger of a consumeristic gospel?
3. What should determine a Christian's worldview?
4. How do you understand what it means to be a "public" Christian?